CW00971095

PROPERTY TYCOON

A SIMPLE SEVEN-STEP GUIDE TO BECOMING A PROPERTY MILLIONAIRE

by Ian Samuels

HARRIMAN HOUSE LTD
3A Penns Road
Petersfield
Hampshire
GU32 2EW
GREAT BRITAIN
Tel: +44 (0)1730 233870

Email: enquiries@harriman-house.com
Website: www.harriman-house.com

First published in Great Britain in 2014.
Copyright © Ian Samuels.

The right of Ian Samuels to be identified as the Author has been asserted in accordance with the Copyright, Designs and Patents Act 1988.

ISBN: 9780857193582

British Library Cataloguing in Publication Data.
A CIP catalogue record for this book can be obtained from the British Library.

 Harriman House

Printed and bound in Great Britain by
Marston Book Services Limited, Oxfordshire

CONTENTS

FREE EBOOK VERSION

As a buyer of the print book of *Property Tycoon* you can now download the eBook version free of charge to read on an eBook reader, your smartphone or your computer. Simply go to:

http://ebooks.harriman-house.com/propertytycoon

or point your smartphone at the QRC below.

You can then register and download your free eBook.

FOLLOW US, LIKE US, EMAIL US

@HarrimanHouse
www.linkedin.com/company/harriman-house
www.facebook.com/harrimanhouse
contact@harriman-house.com

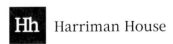 Harriman House

ABOUT THE AUTHOR

HAVING SPENT MORE than 20 years growing a property portfolio, Ian Samuels believes that with the right approach anyone can make a living from investing in property. Ian is an avid student of business, philosophy, sales, management, economics, and human behaviour. He was born in Dublin in 1966 and now lives in Manchester with his wife and two daughters.

WELCOME TO THE WORLD OF PROPERTY INVESTMENT

THIS BOOK IS a step-by-step guide to becoming a successful property investor. With more than 20 years experience in all areas of property I believe this is the most comprehensive guide available on how to become financially free through investing in property.

In starting out investing in property, I was fortunate to have not one but two mentors to guide me on my quest to become a full-time property investor. With their help, I gained the know-how needed to build my own property portfolio. There then followed years of hard graft, learning from success and mistakes what it takes to be successful in buy-to-let property.

Now I want to pass this on. Having built up a portfolio worth millions, and having maintained that portfolio for many years, I want to become a mentor for others and guide them on the same exciting journey. I believe it's one well worth taking.

Since 1990 I have read almost every book on property, been on many courses, and joined numerous property networking groups. Some of these are recommended at the end of this book. None of them offer the complete guide to every aspect of residential buy-to-let *investment*.

There are books out there on being a landlord, and on the ins and outs of the buy-to-let world, and this book certainly covers that material too – but here it's as part of a larger approach, one that is very much focused on property investment from small-scale beginnings all the way up to the point where it can provide substantial and life-changing income.

Most property books stop at the small-scale. I think that means readers miss out. But I do understand the desire to start small and stay small – and if you're just interested in the smaller-scale stuff, this is still the most up-to-date and practical introduction out there on making money from buy-to-let.

But if, like I did, you want to take things further, and see property investment as something that you want to build your wealth around, this book also has you covered.

With *Property Tycoon* I want to provide the ultimate comprehensive guide: one that acts like a mentor, a companion, that can be picked up and referred to at any time for the advice you need, wherever you are on your investing journey.

When starting out I didn't have a plan, I didn't have money, I didn't have any experience and I had little knowledge of buying property. But others helped fill in the gaps – and it's my hope that this book can do the same for you.

Ian Samuels, 2014

This book is dedicated to my late father, who inspired me to write and live life to the full.

A big thank-you to my good friend Clive, for his guidance, years of mentoring and words of wisdom.

To my mum for encouraging me to 'go for it' and follow my dreams. You are an amazing woman. A big thank-you to Simone and Gerry for their love and support, and belief in me – Gerry, you have been a great mentor to me in many ways and for many years.

A huge amount of love and gratitude goes to Marcelle, my wife, for proofreading this book and for her ongoing love and support. Without her this book wouldn't have been possible. And finally to Jessica and Jemma for making me laugh, for inspiring me to get out of bed every morning so I can share my life with them, and for their love and support.

INTRODUCTION: FROM PROPERTY BEGINNER TO INVESTOR

IN 2003, MY wife and I were having supper with four of our best friends over the Christmas holidays. As with many a dinner-party discussion, we were talking about the recent property boom and how house prices had been increasing at an unbelievable pace.

"They can't possibly keep on rising," one friend commented. "I wish I had bought property before the 20% annual increases. Ah well, it's too late now; prices will start coming down soon."

I remember thinking how lucky we were to have four properties under our belt, all benefiting from healthy value increases and rental income. I remember saying to my wife that there would be people all over the country saying something similar to my friend, wishing they had invested in property a few years earlier.

But property prices rose by almost another 20% the following year (2004), and carried on rising for another three years after that.

When that happened, what struck me about our friend's comments was that no one really seemed to be able predict what was going to happen with property prices the following year. This prompted me to truly familiarise myself with the property cycle – the recurring pattern of property values over the long term – and to see if it was possible not be caught out when values rocketed or collapsed.

Something else also struck me about my friend's comments later on. When I look back to that evening, I realise that our conversation was based purely on the capital gain property had experienced in the previous years and not about the potential for good rental gains and the long-term benefits that investing in property offers.

and investing in property is actually even more attractive.

combination of capital *and* rental gain is at the heart of
operty investor. There are other ways to make a living
invesu.. .. in property, and this book provides all the information you
need to pursue them – whether it's buying and letting a couple of flats
in the hope of retiring on their increased value (simply using rent to
cover the mortgages), or looking for bargains that can be renovated
and flipped back onto the market for a quick profit.

But in this book's final chapters, we'll be looking at an approach that
let's you give up the day-job and enjoy significant financial freedom,
and it relies very much on a simple combination of rental yield and
house price value – never being over-reliant on one or the other, and
thus remaining immune from the negative impact of downturns and
void periods.

STABLE, VALUABLE AND IN SHORT SUPPLY

When it comes to investing in property, you can choose to follow the
commercial route or the residential route, or perhaps both. Like most
people I chose residential, which then forks into short-term or long-
term – or 'buy-to-let' vs 'buy-to-sell'. This book is about residential
buy-to-let property investment, the path I've gone down and which I
strongly recommend for others – but those interested in buy-to-sell,
which is a shorter-term strategy, will also be covered by the material
of the first few chapters.

So, why invest in residential property?

- For starters, there is a big shortage of property in the UK and
  an increasing population.

- You can also invest in property using other people's money.

- Over the last 60 years, British property has on average gone up
  in value by approximately 8–9% a year.

- Property doesn't only go up in value in the long term, it also
  provides cash flow in the form of rental income.

If you visit your bank manager and ask for a loan they will want to know what the money is for. If you tell them you want to invest in stocks and shares they won't lend you the money. But they *will* likely lend to you if you wish to borrow the money to purchase a property (providing you have sufficient income and a deposit). That is because banks view property as a long-term and safe investment.

Of all the asset classes one can invest in, property is considered the safest and least volatile. As with any investment vehicle there is always an element of risk involved, but I truly believe that risk in property investment only manifests itself in the *short term*.

Having bought and sold property for more than 20 years, I have made money over two turns of the property cycle. Understanding there is a property cycle just as there is a life cycle or economic cycle, is paramount to building a property portfolio. Most property investors will have studied this cycle and will tune in to it to decide on the most appropriate times to buy or sell. Of course, there are times when we are pressurised into having to buy or sell property, but it helps to know where we are on the cycle if we are going to become serious and successful property investors.

HOW THIS BOOK WILL HELP

This book will take you through seven simple steps to becoming a property millionaire and help you to avoid the mistakes that I made along my path to financial freedom.

There are many books out there about property and property investment, some quite specifically written for those interested in managing and maintaining property, and some written for those keen to buy, do up and sell.

This book is a complete step-by-step guide on *every* aspect of residential property investment, including buying, managing, maintaining, financing and selling ... the complete package. It's for small-scale investors all the way up to those aiming for a substantial property portfolio and a life of passive income.

I will present you with a detailed account of the various stages that take place when purchasing a buy-to-let property, and will also provide various options for securing capital. I will also take you through setting goals, to the types of questions you should ask yourself before making your first purchase.

I want you to view this book as your very own mentor, to refer to it throughout your time as a property investor and when going through the different stages of buying or selling property.

A variety of skills are needed to run and manage a successful property portfolio, and this book will introduce you to all of them – as well as providing information on how to develop them further. But one of the great things about property investment is that you can pick and choose what part of it, and to what extent, you want to be involved.

You may decide to play a partial role in each and all of the steps involved in becoming a property investor, or you may want total control in certain areas and be happy to relinquish responsibility to the 'experts' in others.

Whether you want to manage your own portfolio or have an agent manage it for you, this book will guide you through both scenarios every step of the way and provide you with the advantages and disadvantages for each situation.

THE COMING PROPERTY BOOM

Experience counts for many things and I believe that those who have experienced both the good times and the bad times are better prepared when change does come about. I predict that in 2014–2015 we will enter the next stage of the property cycle and another period of great prosperity, starting with a slow increase in house prices for two to three years, followed by bigger increases in years four to six (2017–2019).

This is one reason I believe that now and within the next couple of years is the best time to invest in property. You don't need to agree with this reason in order to start investing – there are plenty of other reasons to jump in, now or in the future, and they'll be covered throughout this book. In fact, a property cycle by definition means we are never *too* far away from a great time to start investing (though it can feel like it).

But I think there's something to this coming boom, and I think it makes an already interesting prospect all the more alluring.

My father used to remind me of the 'seven years of lean and seven years of plenty' in the story of Joseph in the Bible. He first related this story to me in the late 1980s when a recession hit the UK and most of Europe. He thought this recession would last between six and ten years, and that afterwards a period of prosperity would follow.

Sure enough, approximately eight years later, a period of great economic growth followed and he reminded me of the story again. House prices increased at a phenomenal rate from about 1997, and carried on rising at an unbelievable pace for almost ten years (more than doubling). But my dad warned me again of the recession that would inevitably follow, that once again a period of economic hardship would be upon us.

And here we are right now, nearing the end of that economic slump.

The point is not that the story of Joseph records an inescapable law of macroeconomics. It's that economies are always going through ups and downs – there's a cycle to these things. And house prices invariably come along for the ride in both directions: after all, their mortgages are paid off by those employed in the wider economy.

Countries grow rich, and getting richer, get careless – until the correction comes along. Once reality has bitten, businesses and individuals trim the fat, refocus, get their affairs in order and are perfectly placed to benefit from a recovery – so when a little uplift comes along, economies are primed to motor onwards, and usually do; until, of course, people get too careless again.

If a boom is on the way, that means that anyone reading this book is well placed to start investing in property at the absolute *right* point on the property cycle.

But don't worry. If you disagree – and who could blame you after the last five years of volatility? – the seven steps to becoming a property millionaire outlined in this book do *not* rely on this boom materialising.

I just think it will.

WHY HAVE I WRITTEN THIS BOOK?

In the 22 years I have been dealing in property I have been asked for advice by many people, including family and friends. I have enjoyed offering my help. Having experienced the highs and lows of being a landlord and getting my hands dirty in every aspect of running a property business, I believe nothing beats it. Through the ups and downs – including the recent economic turmoil – I can honestly say I have enjoyed every minute of it and gained a lot from the whole experience.

This has given me a burning desire to put pen to paper and write about what I have learnt. My intention with this book is to give you a detailed guide on how to invest in the property market wisely: whether just dipping in your toe, looking to build a small property portfolio or aiming for a substantial portfolio and significant financial freedom with serious passive income.

Ultimately, with this book I want to be able to guide you to becoming a successful property millionaire. Each of the following chapters will take you through the different steps along the way.

STEP 1.

GETTING STARTED

INTRODUCTION

GETTING STARTED AS a property investor is easier than most people think. Becoming a property investor and entering the buy-to-let business with just one or two properties can be achieved without giving up your day job. It is possible to dip your toe in the water without any major disruption to your daily routine.

If all goes well you can choose whether to expand to create a bigger operation – which could develop into a full-time job – or sell up if you decide it's just not for you.

Before starting out it's important to create the right mindset. Starting a property business is similar in many ways to starting any business. You first need to plan ahead and understand the market you are investing in. Once you have an understanding of how the property market works, and the property cycle itself, you will have a lot more confidence in moving forward and getting started.

Here's what we're going to tackle in *Step 1*:

- questions you should ask yourself at the outset
- setting goals
- planning
- the property cycle.

QUESTIONS YOU SHOULD ASK YOURSELF AT THE OUTSET

1. DO I HAVE WHAT IT TAKES TO BE A PROPERTY LANDLORD?

You may be uncertain whether you have what it takes to become a successful landlord. You can, of course, be a successful property investor while letting someone else manage your properties. If you have a full-time job and you like the idea of investing in property instead of having a pension then you can always just get a letting agent or management company to manage your properties for you.

In order to be a landlord yourself, you should have good people and communication skills. You need to be prepared to do a lot of research about the areas in which you are letting and the type of people you want to rent to. You need to be sceptical and inquisitive and able to manage your finances (though don't worry if you're put off by the property industry's financial jargon – we'll knock that on the head in *Step 2*).

2. WHAT IF I BUY A PROPERTY AT THE WRONG TIME AND THE MARKET DROPS?

Understanding that you are investing for the long term and that over the long term property prices always rise should give you the confidence to buy your first investment property.

Also, understanding the property cycle, and where we are on the cycle at any time, can help you avoid any dips in the market.

Thirdly, remembering you can make money from rental income as well as the capital gain of selling at a higher price is crucial to helping you decide the best properties to purchase.

3. WHERE WILL I FIND THE MONEY TO PAY FOR THE FIRST PROPERTY?

We will cover this in *Step 3: Choosing and Buying Your First Property* and when looking at mortgages in *Step 2*. There are many different ways in which to raise the capital.

4. IS PROPERTY REALLY THE BEST PLACE FOR ME TO INVEST FOR THE FUTURE?

It can be. I certainly think it is, though others are free to disagree with me. You've heard the saying 'safe as houses'. Where better to put your money than in bricks and mortar?

Over the long-term UK property almost always goes up in value and no bank or building society will lend you 80% of the cost to buy any other investment vehicle such as gold or stocks and shares. (I will also explain 'leverage' in a later chapter and the beauty of using other people's money to help you build your portfolio.)

SETTING GOALS

There is a well known saying, '*If you keep doing what you have always done, you will keep getting what you have always got*'. All successful people in life start being successful when they set themselves goals and targets, something to strive for, along with a plan of how they are going to get there.

The same is true for successfully investing in property. It's a big thing and you need to work out in advance what you want to get out of it.

The important thing is not where you were, or where you are, but where you want to get to. Decide where you want to be in five years from now, in ten years from now, and how and what you need to achieve in order to get there. What actions do you need to take now in order to start moving in that direction?

You will face obstacles, but with clear planning and precise goals in mind, you can always overcome them.

The reason for planning is to enable you to transform your definite purpose or goals into a planned strategy with a beginning, middle and end. By setting deadlines you will be motivated into taking appropriate action.

CASE STUDY: Learning to set goals

I have been to many sales seminars and courses on business management, finance, and property over the past 20 years. The one I enjoyed most was a goal-setting course. On that course I learnt how to set goals, decide what it was I wanted to achieve

---

in the short term (the next 12 months), the mid term and long term, and how to go about achieving those targets. Ever since then, I have always set myself goals and targets for the year ahead with a view to achieving as many as possible.

PUTTING YOUR PLAN TOGETHER

Here are some simple questions you can ask yourself to start setting these goals. Don't worry if you don't know how to answer them yet – that's totally fine. After all, we've still got 90% of the book to go. Leave them for now, if you prefer, and come back later. These are just markers to help your thinking while you read and reflect on the rest of the book.

1. Decide on your goal or end result. What do you want to achieve and why? Give this plenty of thought.

2. Write it down. You must be clear and precise in what you want and why. Committing it to paper (or tablet) makes it measurable and real.

3. With targets and goals in mind, set deadlines and sub-deadlines. You may not reach all of these, but you need to measure and track your progress.

4. What are the difficulties and obstacles that stand in your way? Identify them, write them down and think about how you might overcome them.

5. Identify the knowledge and skills you will need to achieve your targets and goals. What do you need to learn and how will you go about gaining this knowledge?

6. Who do you need on your team to help you to achieve your goals? What people and what companies or organisations can help you on your journey? What steps do you need to take to gain the support of these people?

7. Review and revisit your plan every three months.

Don't rush this planning stage. It is important to ensure you have a concise written plan and strategy. Once this is done, you will naturally begin thinking about what action you need to take to start achieving your first target. The only reason I refer to my plan and goal sheet every three months is to see what objectives I have met and to revise certain targets or steps I need to take further down the road.

It is also important to understand that no plan is perfect the first time you create it. You may initially find that you are not reaching any or many of your targets or goals. Don't panic. Adjust the plan. Planning is a skill that can take time to master, but the more you practise the better you will become.

When you do come up against a problem or obstacle, remember what you are trying to achieve and your desired end-result. Set about looking for possible solutions to the problem and think about what steps need to be taken to reach that solution. Break it down into action steps.

CASE STUDY: Creating my first true plan

I remember when I first tried creating a plan. I had been purchasing property for a few years and was fairly clear in my mind what strategy I was following. I just hadn't written down any master plan or short-term strategy and realised the time had come to create one.

My initial strategy was to purchase as many buy-to-let properties as quickly as possible, realising great capital gains in doing so. And that was it. I did not know how I was going to achieve this goal. I did not know if it was even possible.

After a few years of investing in property and after attending the goal-setting course I mentioned just now, I began thinking about the future, and decided that I needed to have a written and testable plan with a short and long-term strategy.

When you create a plan based on your desires, your goals and anticipated opportunities, you are pursuing a deliberate strategy. As mentioned, you will have to modify this strategy as unanticipated problems and opportunities arise. You can choose to continue to follow your deliberate strategy, you can modify your plan or you can even replace it altogether.

CASE STUDY: Reworking a plan in the middle of a crisis

Reworking a plan was forced upon me in 2007–2008 when the economy crashed and property prices dropped. All of a sudden there were no capital gains to enjoy from selling my buy-to-let properties at higher prices than I had bought them for. My strategy needed changing.

Having spent ten years enjoying good capital gains and not focusing too seriously on rental gains, I realised a new phase of the economic cycle had arisen and I would have to adapt.

It took me a while to realise this was actually a golden opportunity. I remember trying to modify and rewrite my short-term strategy many times during 2008 and 2009 while the dust settled. I found it difficult to adjust to the new lending rules imposed on us by the banks, the immediate changes in mortgage-lending and the uncertainty of what was to become of the property market and the UK economy in the following two to three years.

However, it soon became clear that certain opportunities had arisen out of the financial crisis. Because of the increased reluctance to lend money to would-be house-buyers, the rental market surged – *a new buy-to-let era had begun*.

Once I saw this opportunity I was able to see clearly where I was going, planning a new short-term strategy and modifying my long-term strategy.

I like to create a 12-month written plan. I take an A4 piece of paper and divide it into 12 sections, the 12 months of the year. On another piece of paper I write down all the goals I want to achieve in the following year and the steps I need to take to achieve those goals. Then I write my ultimate goal at the end of month 12 and work backwards through month 11, ten and so on, finishing up with month one and the first steps I need to take. Your main concern should be identifying every step necessary, and the time required to accomplish each of these steps.

Remember that it takes time to perfect the planning process. The more careful you are in the planning stage, and the more often you carry out this process, the better you will become at it. The better you are at planning, the more ideas will start to flow and the more creative your mind will become. You will begin achieving bigger and better things.

THE PROPERTY CYCLE

Understanding how the property cycle works is paramount to your planning. In order to look forward and to try and understand what lies ahead for the property market and the economy, you need to look into the past.

UK property prices have more than doubled every ten years since the 1950s. The property cycle in the last 60–70 years has almost always followed the same eight to ten-year cycle: between two to three years of stagnation or small percentage drops in value, followed by four to five years of slow growth and then another two to three years of big growth, sometimes reaching 20–30% in one year.

> The advantage of this regular cycle is that property investors can fairly accurately predict a few years ahead and prepare their finances for a boom or bust period.

WHERE ARE WE NOW?

At the time of writing (early 2014) we have had more than three years of stagnation and falls in property prices, and I believe we are about to enter a period of slow but steady growth lasting two to three years. This is the time to invest in property before we encounter the next stage of the cycle.

In 1988 house prices rose 23% followed by another increase of 20% in 1989. There followed four or five years of stagnation and falling prices, followed by another five or six years of slow but steady growth averaging 5–6%.

Then the huge increases came again in 2002, with a whopping 17% increase in house prices followed by 22% in 2003 and 18% in 2004.

What happened in 2005 was slightly unusual in that house prices continued to rise instead of falling, as they had during previous similar stages of boom and bust cycles. According to the regular property cycle this shouldn't have happened. However, due to the crazy lending situation – with people encouraged to borrow to keep spending, in order to keep the economy ticking along – a big bubble naturally formed.

Between 2005–2007 prices rose steadily when normally they would have fallen, creating the property bubble that in turn caused the big bust of 2007 onwards. So the drop in prices this time round has been deeper and longer than usual – though not as deep as some predicted.

All that means is that, once the market picks up again, we will experience big increases.

So where are we now on the property cycle? Looking at the house price data below, showing how house prices rose and fell between 1984–2012, and taking 2013 into account, we seem about to enter a new period of slow but steady growth sometime between 2014 and 2015.

UK house price data 1984–2013

Year	Index	% change
	100.0	
1984	107.2	7.2
1985	117.0	9.1
1986	129.9	11.0
1987	149.9	15.4
1988	184.8	23.3
1989	223.1	20.8
1990	223.2	0.0
1991	220.5	-1.2
1992	208.1	-5.6
1993	202.1	-2.9
1994	203.1	0.5
1995	199.6	-1.7
1996	208.6	4.5
1997	221.7	6.3
1998	233.7	5.4
1999	250.5	7.2
2000	275.1	9.8
2001	298.6	8.5
2002	350.6	17.4
2003	429.1	22.4
2004	507.6	18.3
2005	536.6	5.7
2006	581.3	8.3
2007	635.9	9.4
2008	585.9	-7.9
2009	524.6	-7.5
2010	539.6	2.9
2011	525.4	-2.6
2012	522.1	-0.6
2013	561.2	+7.5

A note on 2013

The figure of +7.5% in 2013 is actually not a true reflection of what happened to house prices nationwide, as London saw a massive 14% increase and distorted the overall figures. Taking what happened to property prices in London out of the equation, the increase for the rest of the UK was a more moderate +4%.

If you owned a property in the UK in 1983 worth £100,000 and applied the percentage increase or decrease each year, your house could be worth £561,200 in 2013. That is the beauty of compound interest and owning property.

Some so-called experts predicted that the housing market would drop by 30–40% after the economic downturn in 2007. Such a massive drop in prices never materialised and some of these 'experts' still believe house prices are too high and that price-to-income ratios are also too high. I don't think this is right – there are good reasons to believe that such ratios are actually now about normal. I cover this in depth in the book's conclusion for anyone interested in exploring it further.

> **TIP:** Reading the future
>
> **Read as many books about property, old and new, as you possibly can to gain the knowledge needed to anticipate what lies ahead. Understanding the history of the property market, and reading what experienced investors have to say, will always help you in making some tough decisions in the long term.**

SUMMING UP

Once you have made your mind up to invest in property, you are ready to start planning your future as a property investor. Setting goals and having a clearly defined short-term and long-term plan is paramount to making a success of your venture. Understanding the reasons why property is a good long term investment will give you peace of mind and help motivate you to get started.

Also, understanding the property cycle and where we are on the cycle at any given time helps you to plan ahead in buying before the boom period and avoid buying during any bust period.

Some people believe that investing in property is a gamble. However, once you get to grips with the property cycle and learn how to anticipate its various phases, you will learn how to predict what lies ahead and be able to plan the future with some accuracy.

STEP 2.

KNOW YOUR FINANCES

INTRODUCTION

FINANCE IS NOT everyone's favourite subject but it is very important for all property investors to have at least a basic understanding of it. This chapter is intended to be the best pain-free guide to what you need to know. Don't worry – it's not as scary or boring as it's sometimes made out to be.

Above all, you need to be on top of your finances because what is often called 'financing' is critical to any property deal. If the financing package you choose isn't right, despite purchasing the best property in an ideal location you could end up losing money. If you are not somewhat literate on the subject and at least have a fundamental understanding of finance, you will be forced to rely on others for advice when you make decisions about your financial affairs. And that's not a good place to be.

This chapter covers a few essential basics you need to grasp before purchasing your first investment property, such as leverage, debt, capital gain and cash flow, tax, mortgages, income and expenditure, yields, and ROI or return on investment. It will also give you a good insight into some of the basic financial information you should familiarise yourself with before beginning your new property business. You will need to treat your property investment as a business. That is how the authorities will view it.

You might decide that you would prefer to leave the financial side of your business to your accountant, or at least certain aspects of it. Nevertheless, I really think you should still familiarise yourself with the basics so you can make sense of what is going on with the most important part of your investment and understand what your accountant is talking about.

It's just one chapter – and I promise you it's simpler than you think!

LEVERAGE

What is leverage? In simple terms, leverage is the use of borrowed money to increase the potential return of an investment. The more you borrow, the greater the leverage.

Property is all about leverage. When you are purchasing a property, the bank will lend you 70%, 80% or even 90% of the money you need.

So let's say you have £40,000 of spare capital and you're looking to make an investment. You look at shares and you look at property. To buy £40,000 worth of shares, you need £40,000. (Using a high-risk alternative such as spread betting would change this, but that's getting away from investing so I won't include it here.)

That same £40,000, however, could instead be used as a deposit for a property worth £200,000.

The bank would then lend you the other 80% you need (£160,000) in the form of a mortgage. Now your total investment is worth £200,000 as opposed to £40,000. If the property and the shares both go up 10%, you would only make £4,000 from the increase in the share price, but your property investment would be worth an extra £20,000.

Now let's say there is a 20% increase in the share price and the property price over a period of one year; your shares will have increased by £8,000, whereas your property has now made you a profit of £40,000.

At this point you could turn to your mortgage lender and borrow another £30,000 from the growth of your investment to use as a deposit to purchase a second property.

This is the power of leverage. I will cover this in more detail later in the book when we look at financing and growing your portfolio

2013	2014 (20% increase)
Shares worth £40,000	Shares worth £48,000 (£8,000 profit)
Property worth £200,000	Property worth £240,000 (£40,000 profit)

Some might argue that you have to pay the bank interest on your £160,000 loan. However, this will – rather marvellously – be covered by tenants paying you rent for your property.

GOOD DEBT / BAD DEBT

Before we look at borrowing in order to purchase our first investment property and the various options available to us, it is important to understand the difference between good debt and bad debt. Debt is simply a sum of money owed. Debt can be thought of as inevitably bad. But I learnt many years ago that there is good debt and bad debt and that *good* debt is very much a positive thing.

If a debt is simply an amount of money owed, then your mortgage is a debt. So is a car you buy on a hire-purchase agreement, as is using your credit card to buy something. When you apply for any form of credit to buy something you will normally be asked what debts you have. If you want to take out a mortgage or borrow further on your existing mortgage, the bank or building society will ask you what other debts you hold before making a decision as to whether to lend you more money.

Part of the problem that snowballed out of the era of reckless lending by the banks was the build up of bad debt by a large part of society: banks and building societies offering 100% mortgages and in some cases 125% mortgages, without taking out the necessary financial checks. This resulted in many households and families facing serious debt problems and negative equity when the economy collapsed, with the market value of their property falling to less than the amount of their mortgage.

Bad debt like this kills property investing. We want to avoid it at all costs.

The government and the banks were partly responsible in trying to boost consumer spending. As far as the government was concerned, consumerism was keeping the economy motoring and therefore, as long as we all believed that house prices would carry on rising, we could carry on spending – putting an end to boom and bust. I say they and the banks were 'partly responsible', as people must also take responsibility for their own actions.

I recently applied for additional borrowing on one of my mortgages and was asked for a list of all my debts. I have many debts, as every mortgage counts as a debt. However, in the eyes of the lender, mortgage debt is good debt. This is because the asset can always be taken back from you if you can't afford to keep paying it off.

Mortgages with ridiculous loans-to-value (LTV) like 100–125%, however, are nothing but bad debts for the people who hold them. For the same reason: the asset can be taken away from them.

> So any money borrowed (sensibly) and used to invest in assets is good debt, but any money borrowed for a holiday, or to purchase a car with, or any other liabilities, is bad debt.

Since the crash of 2007–2008 the banks and building societies have pulled their 100% and 125% LTV offers. As so many people ended up in negative equity, it isn't difficult to understand why such crazy deals are no longer available. If you purchased a property for £200,000 in 2007 with a 100% mortgage and property prices dropped 15% then your house would be worth £170,000, and you would find yourself in £30,000 negative equity.

Because property prices can go down as well as up you should always work in a buffer of at least 10–15%. This is really, really important, no matter how big or small your property investing is going to be. It's vital to protect yourself from bad debt. If you want to purchase a buy-to-let property I would *always* recommend putting down at least a 10% deposit to allow for a drop in house prices.

A bank won't repossess a property as long the mortgage is being repaid. A bank will only consider repossessing a property if the monthly payments cease to be made. If the owner is unable to make these payments and has built in a 10–15% buffer then they can sell the property and still have some equity left provided prices haven't come down more than this 10–15%. Even if prices have dropped by this amount and the owner is unable to keep up repayments they can still sell up without having their property repossessed by the bank. If property prices fall by more than 10–15% and mortgage payments are not met, then the bank might repossess.

Fortunately, as a result of the recent turmoil, most lenders currently won't lend more than 80% for buy-to-let properties. Needless to say, once the market picks up and the economy begins to grow at a reasonable pace again, lenders will become a little less stringent. Don't get sucked in.

CAPITAL GAIN AND CASH FLOW

Cash flow is vitally important to the survival and development of your portfolio. Without a good cash flow strategy and discipline you are doomed to fail.

In the previous chapter I wrote about strategy and the importance of planning ahead. When I purchased my first buy-to-let property I only had a long-term plan and that was to make a profit from the capital gain of selling a house at a higher price.

This was fine as long as property continued to increase in value. What I hadn't allowed for or even thought about was what would happen if prices started to drop. This is where experience lends a hand. Having experienced the economic downturn in 2007, I realised a new strategy was needed and that rental income and cash flow should play a *big* part in my short-term strategy from that point on.

Capital gain and cash flow are the two primary reasons we should buy property. Managing the two together is not easy and it's this management and control of cash flow and capital that is paramount to growing your property portfolio. If you do not manage the cash flow and you start missing mortgage payments, the likelihood is you will have your property repossessed. So from the outset you should keep a record of all purchase costs, rental income, mortgage payments and other expenses – that way you'll know what's going on with your cash flow at any one time.

Cash flow for property investors is, in simple terms, money you receive in rent. This needs to be spent on mortgages, insurance, maintenance and other outlays such as service charges (for leasehold properties) and ground rent. On your end-of-year tax return all this will appear as 'Income and Expenditure', which we will come to later in this chapter. You have positive cash flow when the rental income is *more* than all your outgoings, and a negative cash flow where your rental income is *less* than your outgoings/expenses.

Capital gain is simply the growth or gain of your investment when you decide to sell; what it is worth over and above what you paid for it.

In *Step 6: Developing Your Portfolio*, I will give a more detailed analysis of capital gain and cash flow and how, if managed well, they can work together to give you great capital gains at the same time as long-term passive income. I will also explain how to grow and expand your portfolio by managing and controlling your cash flow.

TAX

Her Majesty's Revenue and Customs (HMRC) is quite kind to property investors, and there are certain tax advantages property investors benefit from when they understand how the system works.

Because the tax laws change quite regularly, I would recommend checking the HMRC website at **www.hmrc.gov.uk** to keep up to date with all the changes and updates.

The two main taxes you need to be aware of as a property investor are capital gains and income tax.

When you do your tax return you need to write down all your property income from letting and all your costs. The tax year runs from 6 April to 5 April of the following year. Costs and income should be accounted for in the tax year when the bill is incurred as opposed to when it is paid. For example, if you have a roof repair in March 2015, receive the invoice in the same month, but pay the invoice in May 2015 (after the end of the tax year), then you should deduct the costs for the tax year ending April 2015 as opposed to April 2016.

> If you have received a lot of rental income and end the year with a big profit after costs, and you have a big costly repair to carry out, try to get this in before the tax year ends as this will lower your tax liability.

Rent money is income, so naturally you will be liable to pay income tax on the profit you make. Property letting is treated like any other business for income tax purposes.

Before getting into the buy-to-let business it is important to understand how to prepare your accounts at the end of the tax year, showing all your income and expenditure. As part of that you need to know what will be allowable as a deductible expense – in other words, what can lower your tax bill. Below is a list of some of those allowable expenses:

- The mortgage interest you pay plus other finance costs (if you take out a separate loan to pay for the deposit then this is also allowable)
- accountancy fees
- letting agents' fees
- buildings insurance
- repairs and renewals (maintenance costs but not home improvements)
- ground rent and service charges
- utility bills (if you are paying them)
- services such as gardening or cleaning (if you are paying for those services)
- wear-and-tear allowance if you furnish the property
- advertising for tenants
- other costs you might incur in the general management of your properties such as phone calls, petrol/diesel to and from the property, office and stationery costs etc.

TIP: Wear and tear

I claim the 10% wear-and-tear allowance each year. This is 10% of the annual rent received. When starting out you have the choice to claim this 10% wear-and-tear allowance each year, or to claim it as a total cost or replacement when you purchase. *Once you have chosen how to claim your furniture allowance you cannot switch.*

The beauty is that any costs incurred in buying property or in the upkeep of your property are all tax-deductible. Any money you invest or re-invest into your portfolio can be offset against your rental income. So if you re-mortgage a let property, the interest on any extra borrowing you then use to purchase another property with is tax-deductible. Providing you use that extra borrowing to re-invest for property purposes, and you can prove it, you will also be allowed to deduct the interest. This might include installing a new replacement kitchen, replacing a rotten roof, or even buying new furniture.

CAPITAL IMPROVEMENT (CAPITAL EXPENDITURE) OR REPAIR (REVENUE EXPENDITURE)

There is one grey area when it comes to your tax return: deciphering what is a repair/renewal, and what is a capital improvement. When a property first becomes recognised as a rental property – that is, when it is first let or purchased for rental purposes – any expenditure incurred to make it fit for renting will be deemed capital expenditure and therefore is not tax deductible.

A new extension will be classified as an 'enhancement' and therefore a capital improvement; again, non-deductible.

If you are making a repair to this 'rental property' then it is tax-deductible and you should be clear in your mind that it is a repair. If you are having a new kitchen fitted, replacing a previous similar set of units, worktops etc, then this would be accepted as repair expense. This would include the costs for re-tiling, plastering, plumbing, electrical work etc.

If a new improved kitchen with all mod cons is fitted, replacing a sub-standard older kitchen, then an appropriate proportion of the expenditure will need to be treated as a capital improvement.

CASE STUDY: An allowable bathroom

A few years ago I had to replace an old bathroom that was in poor condition. There was a leak in the hallway downstairs and the floor in the bathroom was starting to sag. I thought it was a good time to rip the whole bathroom out and replace it with a similar but new bathroom.

Because a bathroom is considered part of the fabric of the building, repairing or replacing it is allowable for tax purposes. If I make new additions such as a new bathroom cabinet, an extractor fan, a shower that wasn't present before, then these additions will be seen as a capital improvement and therefore not allowable as a repair or renewal.

There are many different scenarios where it will be difficult to argue what is a capital improvement and what is a repair or renewal. I have had arguments with my accountant about these issues in the past, and will probably continue to do so. What you need to be clear about is whether you can genuinely argue that you have made a repair. If you put it on your tax return as a repair and you know it is a capital improvement, you may run into trouble with the tax inspector if they start asking questions.

RENTAL LOSSES

If at the end of the tax year you can show a loss made from your property business, you can carry this loss forward and set it off against future rental profits, perhaps the following year. You can carry these losses over for as long as you continue to have a UK property rental business.

CAPITAL GAINS TAX

In 2004, just over a year after purchasing them, I sold two two-bedroom houses and made a profit of £27,000 on the first, and £30,000 on the second. After capital gains tax and legal costs I cleared about £44,000. Capital gains tax (CGT) is a government tax payable on the sale of a property where the property has been sold for a higher price than it was purchased for. Likewise, if a property is transferred to anyone other than a spouse, the person making the transfer becomes liable to pay CGT as if they were selling the property.

This tax is paid on the gain made and is only payable in the case of an investment property; you do not pay CGT when you sell your own main residential home.

CGT can be as much as 28%, although there are certain reliefs that can be applied to reduce the amount of tax that is due.

The annual tax-free allowance (known as the annual exempt amount) allows you to make a certain amount of gains each year before you have to pay tax. Nearly everyone who is liable to capital gains tax gets this tax-free allowance.

There's one annual exempt amount for:

- most individuals who live in the UK
- executors or personal representatives of a deceased person's estate
- trustees for disabled people.

Most other trustees get a lower annual exempt amount.

ANNUAL EXEMPT AMOUNTS

Customer group	2014–15	2015–16
Individuals, personal representatives and trustees for disabled people	£11,000	£11,100
Other trustees	£5,550	TBC

I always purchase property with my wife so we are joint owners. Because every individual has an annual CGT allowance, we therefore benefit from two lots of the annual exempt amount (2014: £11,000 + £11,000 = £22,000).

CAPITAL GAINS TAX RATES

For 2014–15, the following capital gains tax rates apply:

- 18% and 28% for individuals (the rate used will depend on the amount of their total taxable income and gains)
- 28% for trustees or personal representatives.

Applying the annual exempt amounts and CGT rate to the profits I made when selling the two properties in 2004, I worked it out as follows:

- Profit after selling two properties: £57,000
- Less legal costs and cost for selling: £3,000
- Less annual CGT allowance: £8,200 (2004-2005 CGT allowance) × 2 (me and my wife)

    57,000 - 3,000 - 16,400 = 37,600

This left a total of £37,600 to be taxed at 28% = £10,528.

That would be the tax payable after the sale of both properties.

There are other reliefs enabling you to reduce the amount of CGT payable and I could write a complete chapter just on this topic. However, it is a very complex and complicated topic, so I will leave this subject with the basic explanation above. For a more detailed explanation of CGT and property tax in general, I recommend reading the book by Carl Bayley: *How to Avoid Property Tax*.

Carl Bayley is a tax specialist and every year revises his book to include all the new laws and changes to the tax system. He writes a very detailed account and a complete chapter on capital gains tax and I have referred to his book every year when putting together my end of year accounts. You can of course also visit the HM Revenue & Customs website (**www.hmrc.gov.uk**) to obtain an understanding of the rates and allowances.

MORTGAGES

A buy-to-let mortgage is quite different from a residential mortgage and it really is worth doing some research and shopping round for the best buy-to-let mortgage offers. In recent years many lenders have created special buy-to-let divisions to cater for the surge in people buying second and third homes to rent.

BASICS

MORE COSTLY

Buy-to-let mortgages are more costly than residential mortgages by about 1%. The lender will also charge you higher fees for the mortgage. Typical fees can be 1–3% of the amount you borrow. This fee can be added to the mortgage so you do not have to pay it upfront. They will also charge you a valuation fee which can vary between £250 to £450.

RENTAL POTENTIAL

Another difference with a buy-to-let mortgage is that the amount the lender is willing to lend you is not only determined by the amount you earn. The buy-to-let market has different criteria for lending and the lender will want to know the rental potential of the property. On average the rental should be 125–130% of the annual interest payments.

If you purchase a property for £150,000 and put down a 20% deposit (£30,000), you will end up with a mortgage of £120,000. If you are paying 5% interest on this loan, your monthly payments will be £500. You will therefore need to convince the lender that you will get a rental income of £650 a month (30% higher than the monthly interest payments).

The lender will send a surveyor out to value the property at the same time as estimating what the property might achieve in rental income. This system works well and I have never had a problem with the lender not estimating the same rental income I predict. Providing you are realistic in your predictions, the lender will nearly always agree.

OTHER FACTORS

If you already have a few buy-to-let properties, then the lender will take other factors into consideration before agreeing to lend to you. Your income from any job you have will come into play as will your gearing (the ratio of debt or loan capital to the value of equity – a measure of financial leverage), and how many buy-to-let mortgages you have. Any lender is likely to check your current borrowing versus current rental income.

For example, if you have a high gearing of 70% or above (where your borrowing is greater than 70% of the total value of your property portfolio), they may consider you too much of a risk. Some lenders steer clear of any landlords with more than three or four properties. Fortunately, because the buy-to-let market is so competitive this won't stop you getting someone to lend to you.

Shop around when searching for the best mortgage. Check the papers, check out what offers the lenders are offering on the internet, and ask your bank what they have to offer. It is a very competitive market and sometimes it's easy to get confused with all the various mortgages and different options out there.

FIND A GOOD MORTGAGE BROKER!

The buy-to-let market is mainly conducted through intermediaries and about 90% of investors use a mortgage broker to obtain finance. Brokers have access to a full range of buy-to-let lenders, a number of whom won't deal directly with mortgage clients.

So I personally recommend trying to find a good mortgage broker who will do the legwork for you. If you do not know a good one, ask friends or anyone you know who recently moved house if they can recommend one. The advantage of using a reputable and established broker is that they are mostly independent and therefore not biased in their views. They will earn a commission from the lender and in some cases charge you a one off fee of 0.5–1% of the loan. Once you use them more regularly and start recommending them to friends, they might even lower their fees, earning their commission just from the lender.

This is a great win-win scenario, as the service becomes free and the broker is benefiting from referrals. My broker sources all my mortgages for me and has been recommended to many friends.

Even if you do use a broker, make sure you read all the small print and look out for things like penalty clauses and early redemption charges. You can be charged up to 4 or 5% of the loan if you decide to sell or move to another better mortgage deal before the term has expired. A good broker should point these clauses and other important points out to you.

I prefer to take out interest-only mortgages in order to keep my outgoing cash flow low, and the repayment terms on a repayment loan work against you when it comes to your tax liability at the end of the year (more on this later).

FIXED RATES

This is a tough one to decide on, and totally depends on your view on how interest rates will play out in the following few years. If you believe interest rates will stay low for the foreseeable future or for at least a year or two then it might be wise to opt for a variable rate as these are set lower than fixed rates. On the other hand if you are unsure which way rates will go then it is wise to fix. By fixing for a period of two or three years you will know what your payments will be during this time and be able to plan ahead. I prefer to fix for this reason.

VARIABLE RATES

Obviously variable rates can go up or down so you do need to be careful and allow for an increase in your monthly payments if opting for a variable rate. If you decide to opt for a variable rate try to find one without penalties so you can jump ship and transfer over to a fixed rate if you suddenly feel rates are going to rise.

TRACKER RATES

A tracker rate simply tracks the base rate (the interest rate set by the Bank of England at which it lends to financial institutions). Again, make sure when a mortgage broker talks about tracking the base rate it means the Bank of England base rate. A few years ago when the base rate was about 4 to 5%, certain lenders were offering tracker rate mortgages 0.5% **below** the base rate – unheard of in years past. Needless to say, once the interest rates started dropping these rates were pulled by the lenders. If you were fortunate enough to have one of these trackers at 0.5% below the base rate for a two-year period, you would have been paying nothing on your mortgage while the base rate was +0.5% and you were still within the two-year deal.

As the Bank of England base rate started dropping in 2008, lenders began offering less attractive tracker rates such as 1.5% above the base rate. In 2008–2009 this didn't seem like such a good deal compared with what had been on offer the previous year. However, looking back now, if you managed to fix on a tracker rate of anything close to 1.5% above base you were doing very well indeed.

At the time of writing, tracker rates are very popular because the Bank of England is not expected to raise the base rate until the latter part of 2014 or even into 2015. More than half buy-to-let mortgages taken out in 2012 were low-cost bank-rate trackers, even though the average tracker rate is set at 3.3% above the base rate. This is now considered a good deal.

EXTRA BORROWING ON YOUR FAMILY HOME

If you decide to re-mortgage your family home in order to release some equity to purchase your first buy-to-let property, that extra borrowing will need to be separated from your existing mortgage.

For example, if you have a £100,000 repayment mortgage where you are paying back capital as well as interest and you wish to borrow another £40,000 on interest-only terms, your bank or mortgage lender will keep your existing £100,000 mortgage as it is, and set up a new separate mortgage loan for the extra £40,000 on an interest-only basis. This then makes it clear to everyone, including HMRC, that you have borrowed the extra money on different terms for a different purpose.

When you prepare your end-of-year tax return you can then include the interest payments for this extra loan on your expenditure side. A few years later, and if your family home has increased in value again, then you might be able to apply for further borrowing and add it to the existing interest-only loan.

TIP: Tax

When taking out further borrowing on your own property, arrange for the new funds obtained to be allocated to a separate mortgage loan account with the bank. Make the new extra loan interest-only whilst leaving the original mortgage as a repayment account.

In order to obtain a mortgage or loan from the bank you will need to have a good credit score or credit rating. You can check this yourself on the Experian website: **www.experian.co.uk**.

As long as you pay your bills on time and do not have large outstanding credit card bills or overdue loans, you should be able to obtain a mortgage or loan from the banks and building societies.

Not all banks and building societies provide mortgages for landlords, but there are many lenders out there who do. Most lenders will want to know the anticipated rental income from the property you are trying to obtain a mortgage for, to calculate whether there will be more than enough income to cover the mortgage costs along with other costs you might have.

When the lender values the property they will also ask the surveyor to report what rent he thinks the property can achieve. Normally the lender will want the rent to be 1.25 times greater than the interest payments on the mortgage loan. If your mortgage interest is £500 then you will want the surveyor to report an expected rental income of at least £625 a month.

Another thing to watch out for is the early redemption penalty. This is a penalty charge you will incur if you end the mortgage early. If you are thinking of selling a property within one or two years, then make sure you read the small print and avoid a mortgage with an early redemption clause. Remember most lenders currently charge astronomical fees and these can be added to the mortgage. As a rule of thumb I add £2,000 to £3,000 to the cost of the property when purchasing. So if a house is costing me £150,000 then in my mind I am purchasing it for £153,000. This helps to ease the pain of paying the mortgage application fee.

INTEREST-ONLY MORTGAGES VS REPAYMENT MORTGAGES

You can't deduct interest and capital on your tax return. If you opt for a repayment mortgage – where you are paying back some of the capital and interest – then you will need to separate these out so you only deduct the interest payments. Your mortgage provider should send you an annual statement each tax year, showing how much was paid in interest and how much was repayment of the capital.

Most professional landlords I know opt for interest-only mortgages. With a repayment mortgage you are paying back the capital and interest, which means the loan amount is becoming lower every year and therefore so is the interest. This in turn means you will make a higher profit each year from the rental income, and therefore be liable for a higher tax bill at the end of the year.

For example: if the rental income for the year is £9,600, the interest is £6,600 and other costs add up to £2,000, then the taxable income is £1,000.

However, if you have a repayment mortgage and are paying off the capital as well as the interest and after a few years you have cleared half the mortgage loan, then the interest will also be half, equalling £3,300. If you are still getting rental income of £9,600 less the £2,000 costs and £3,300 interest, then £4,300 is now taxable income as opposed to £1,000. You will therefore be paying a lot more tax at the end of the year.

KEEPING TAXABLE INCOME DOWN – AN ASIDE

There is an argument both ways when it comes to keeping your borrowing high and your interest and costs high in order to keep your taxable income low. What if interest rates increase and you have a tracker mortgage which tracks the base rate? You might end up with no taxable income and a loss. What happens if you have some unexpected extra costs and again end up showing a loss at the end of the year? There are other scenarios such as a void period with no tenants, or a drop in house prices.

The flip-side to this argument is that with no profit showing at the end of the year and rental profit wiped out by high mortgage payments and other costs, there will be little or no taxable income to pay. Some landlords I know sail very close to the wind and prefer this scenario; they're ultimately only interested in profiting from the sale of the house. Other landlords I know rely on rental income as their main source of income, and therefore try to maximise their rental income while keeping costs as low as possible.

The following table is an example of an income and expenditure statement for a year-end tax return. It should show all your rental income for the year and all your outgoings.

Example income and expenditure for year-end tax purposes

Accounts prepared for Property No.1, Milton Street, Manchester

	Income	Expenditure
Rent	7,200	
Rent, rates, insurance, ground rent		400
Repairs, renewals and maintenance		700
Finance charges (loan interest)		3,600
Accountancy costs		150
Services (gardening and cleaning costs)		100
Letting charges		545
10% wear-and-tear allowance		720
Total	7,200	6,215

This means you will be liable to pay tax on the profit you have made from your rental income after all your expenses; in this case, £985. If you are a 20% tax payer you will have to pay £197 for this particular property. If you have five properties, you would add up all your rental income and subtract all your costs for the year for all five properties.

I try to purchase at least one property every year and I know other landlords who do the same in order to reduce their tax liability. When you purchase a property you will incur some big extra costs, such as repair or renovation work, legal and professional fees, or loan arrangement fees.

This is an important part of managing your property portfolio and it is important to get it right, so I do advise that you get yourself a good accountant to help you in the first year or two to ensure you are calculating everything in the correct way. But make sure any accountant you do use is up to speed with all the tax laws involving property, and ask for advice in case you are missing something.

For income tax purposes, a vacant property that you intend to sell is no longer classified as a rental property once you have taken that decision to sell it.

DO THE MATHS

When you are planning to purchase your first buy-to-let property you should think of it as a business. The rental income you receive should be more than all your monthly outgoings. I try to ensure that the rental income is at least 20% to 30% above the monthly costs.

Example

Monthly income	Monthly costs
Rent £600	Mortgage £322
	Service charge £80
	Maintenance £50
Monthly profit = £148	

RENTAL YIELD

Rental yield is the annual rental return from a property, or the amount of rent the property earns over a year. It is expressed as a percentage of the purchase price.

You will often hear the term rental yield once you become a property investor and start to rent out your property. It is important to work out the rental yield on a property before you purchase, to help you decide whether it is a good investment. It's an important tool for all serious property investors, and is also used to make comparisons between different properties. Perhaps one property promises a gross yield of 5%, whereas the other property offers a more attractive 6.5%.

If you calculate your rental yield to be 6.5%, then you can decide whether you would be better off investing your money elsewhere or in another property with a higher yield.

The simplest way to calculate rental yield is to work out all your monthly costs, then subtract this figure from your rental income, and multiply by 12 to give you your annual profit. Now divide that figure by the cost of the property and multiply by 100 to give you a percentage.

Example

Property cost (2 bed flat)	£120,000
One off purchase costs including arrangement fees	£2,500
Total investment	**£122,500**
Monthly rent	£600
Annual rental income	£7,200
Less expected annual costs	£600
Total income less expenses or costs	£6,600
Gross income yield a year	**5.4%**
Mortgage loan (£90,000 + £2,500 fees)	£92,500
Annual mortgage costs	£3,875
Annual Service charge costs	£960
Annual rental income after expenses	£1,765
Initial investment for purchase 25%	£30,000
Mortgage arrangement fee and legal fees	£2,500
(Capital investment)	£32,500
Net income yield / annum	**5.4%**

Gross income yield = income after expenses divided by total investment × 100

Net income yield = income after expenses less mortgage costs, divided by initial investment × 100

In order to calculate these figures exactly you should also include one-off costs you might incur when purchasing the property such as any books you read for research, any travel costs to and from the property, a survey cost, stamp duty etc.

What yield should you look for? Well, that will depend on a few factors. However, I try to look for at least 5% and anything over 6% I view as quite positive. The national average yield was 4.8% in 2010, 5.1% in 2011 and 6.4% in 2012, so we are on an upward trend and that figure is expected to rise again in 2013 (final figures not published until early 2014) as rents are expected to keep rising.

RETURN ON INVESTMENT

You will also hear the term **ROI** or **return on investment**. This is one of my favourites. Determining your return on investment is a very important part of any investment review. Whether you're investing in savings accounts, stocks, property or new business ventures, estimating a return on investment will aid you in choosing among investment options.

Simply put, return on investment is the *growth* of your initial investment divided by the initial investment × 100, divided by a certain number of years; in this case, let's say five years.

If you purchased the property for £120,000 (using the figures from a moment ago), and you expect a 5% increase in value each year for five years, then the property will be worth £153,154 in five years' time. Now deduct the mortgage, which in this case is interest-only, so £92,500. This leaves us with £60,654. This £60,654 is now the calculated future value of your investment. The growth of your initial investment is £28,154 (£60,654 less your original capital investment of £32,500).

In order to work out the ROI, divide this initial investment growth of £28,154 by your initial capital investment of £32,500. This gets us 0.87. For the percentage, times this by 100. Then divide the result by five to get the result over five years. We get 17.32% a year.

SUMMING UP

The more financial knowledge you have, the better prepared you will be to run your property business. I can't stress enough the importance of obtaining at least a basic understanding of finance and how it all works. When I started out, I barely had a basic understanding and realised soon enough that I needed to learn fast. I bought many books about property and finance in order to grasp what my accountant was talking about.

Even if you do decide to hand over the reins to a financial advisor, remember it is your money and you still have ultimate responsibility. Your financial advisor may know more than you, so let them guide you and make suggestions – but you, and only you, should make the final decisions.

Before purchasing your first investment property it's important to understand that there are a whole range of taxes that apply to property and understanding these taxes and how they work is crucial to building your property portfolio.

Once you have got to grips with the basics and appreciate how leverage works, and the importance of controlling capital gain and cash flow, you are well-prepared. Still, in the initial years of building your portfolio I recommend using a good accountant or financial advisor and a good mortgage broker as part of your team. More on this in *Step 4*.

STEP 3.

CHOOSING AND BUYING YOUR FIRST PROPERTY

INTRODUCTION

BUYING PROPERTY TO rent out to someone else is very different to buying a property for yourself. You will need to have a completely different mindset and will need to make some tough decisions without any emotion.

Before deciding which property to purchase it's important to decide whether you are investing for capital gain, rental yield – or, in a growth market, both. By making the right decisions early on – carefully thought out and well researched – you are more likely to make a positive and profitable start to your new property business.

This step will take you through the various stages of buying your first property, financing a property, choosing the best location, finding a property that suits the needs and wants of the market you have chosen to let to, choosing the right mortgage and how to go about finding tenants.

FROM INTEREST TO COMPLETION

What are the various stages in buying an investment property? The process usually looks a little like this:

1. THE SUMS

Do the sums, work out how much you can afford as a deposit. You will need to speak to a mortgage broker, either an independent broker who has been recommended or your bank's mortgage advisor, who will help you work out how much you can afford to borrow, how much your monthly payments might be on an interest-only loan or repayment loan, and to find out what mortgage offers are available.

2. MAKING AN OFFER

Once you have registered an interest in a property and decided you wish to make an offer, you will need to decide what solicitor/conveyancer you will want to represent you. Shop around, ask for quotes and try to get recommendations. A good, reputable solicitor/conveyancer can make the difference between a smooth or a stressful property purchase. Their role is to carry out the legal process of buying and selling property, which includes: local searches, land charges search, land registry, and stamp duty. As soon as you place an offer on a property the estate agent will ask you for your conveyancer's details to pass on to the seller's conveyancer.

You may wish to negotiate and offer lower than the asking price for an investment property. Once the negotiation process is complete and a price has been agreed, you will need to give your solicitor's details to the agent selling the property. You will also need to let your mortgage broker know that you have agreed a price so they can sort out your mortgage application. At this point in time, your solicitor should start drawing up a contract.

3. SURVEYING

The survey. Your lender will then value the property within a few days of agreeing the mortgage in principle. As mentioned previously, this will be a basic valuation as opposed to a thorough survey. There are three types of house survey: a basic survey costing £150 to £200, a homebuyer's survey or report costing £250 to £450, and a full structural survey costing £400+. I recommend the middle option, a home-buyer's report as this is a fairly comprehensive survey and will certainly pick up on any major problems with the property including any structural issues.

If there are any serious structural problems, and you have some concerns as to whether to proceed with the purchase, then you can always instruct a full structural survey before proceeding with the sale. Any decent surveyor will be able to spot if there are any structural issues and will advise you further on this matter.

Read the survey thoroughly and if there are any problems with the property that will incur extra costs, it is essential to go back to the agent to try to re-negotiate the price. The survey might suggest that you get quotes for certain work that needs doing, in which case you should do this before re-negotiating.

4. THE DEPOSIT

After your solicitor or conveyancer has completed all the necessary checks, you'll be asked to sign a contract legally committing you to the purchase. At this point you will need to pay a deposit for the property, usually 5 to 10% of the agreed price. After this, you will usually agree a date to complete the sale.

5. GETTING INSURED

Your mortgage broker or lender should advise you at this stage to take out buildings insurance for the property from the agreed completion date.

6. GETTING THE KEYS

Completion. You will be advised when completion has taken place and your solicitor will inform you that the keys are ready for collection from the agent.

WHAT AREA SHOULD I START LOOKING IN?

Location is important when buying any property. But what areas should you start looking in and what type of property should you buy?

If you are just starting out, I would recommend starting in an area close to where you live; somewhere you're familiar with. You don't have to limit yourself to this, but it can give you a bit of a head start. It enables you to draw on your knowledge of the local area and to be close by to deal with any problems.

The ideal property is one that will rent *quickly* and that will give you a good *rental return*. I also look for property that I believe will give good capital growth – i.e. value increase over time. Thankfully, the reasons for a good rental return and good capital growth are often the same.

An investment property should ideally be: close to schools, shops and transport (local and national – tenants may not have cars). The area should be safe and well-lit and low in crime (check **www.neighbourhood.statistics.gov.uk**). You should talk to local people to gain as much information about an area as possible. If feasible, you want to be in a town or city near good restaurants and bars; at least within walking distance.

Talk to as many letting agents and estate agents in the area as possible. If more than one local agent gives you the same information then you can be fairly sure it's accurate. Note how long certain properties stay on the market and how quickly they rent. It won't take more than a few weeks to get a feel for whether an area is strong for rentals or not. By doing the research you will notice what type of properties rent faster and what would-be tenants are looking for when renting.

You can, of course, check out lots of different websites to help you with your research – **www.rightmove.co.uk/property-to-rent** is as good a place as any to start. Here Rightmove lists all the properties that local agents have listed for renting; it's a great source of information.

Local landlords, if you can find any, are also an ideal source of information. Likewise, joining local property networking groups is a great way of finding out what areas are best for rentals. I am a member of one such group that meets in Manchester once a month. I still find it amazing how much you can learn talking to likeminded property investors at these meetings.

Lastly, you should also check out local newspapers. They will often give you a good indication as to whether there is strong rental demand in an area.

WHAT TYPE OF PROPERTY SHOULD I INVEST IN?

Novice landlords often make the mistake of buying a house or flat that they would like to live in themselves, rather than choosing a location and property that provides the best return.

There is not much point in buying a big family home with four bedrooms in an area where there are few families looking to rent large houses. Talk to the local letting agent and ask them what properties they get most demand for. It's a lot easier to rent out a two-bedroom apartment or three-bed semi than it is to rent out a large four-bed detached property.

You might think it always makes more sense to purchase, say, a two-bedroom apartment as it costs less than a three-bed house, but you must remember to take other factors and costs into account. The apartment might see you facing a £1,200 annual service charges or it could be a leasehold property with only 80 years left on the lease. Do some research.

When purchasing a buy-to-let property it is obviously paramount to ensure it is in the right area for rentals, but you should also be asking yourself whether you will be able to sell it easily and quickly if you decide to sell years later.

This is another time for number-crunching. When deciding what type of property is the one to buy, make sure you will get a good rental yield as well as potential for capital growth. And don't let the local agent fool you into believing you can get £950 a month rent for that three-bed semi when the going rate is actually only £850. Or £600 for the two-bed flat when the going rate is really only £500. Try to talk to other landlords in the area and check out advertisements to see what landlords are advertising their properties for.

TIP: It's the little things
There are some small things you should always check during your property-hunting process. They're easy to overlook, but only take a minute. Firstly, check out car-parking facilities. Some flats do not guarantee a parking space and most tenants will want to park their car as close to the property as possible. It is also easier to sell and rent a first floor flat than a ground floor or basement flat for security reasons. And if it's a third or fourth floor flat, is there a lift? Lastly, is the property on a flight path?

Should you specialise in houses or flats? Or look to balance the two in your portfolio? Or not care either way? Some investors prefer one or the other. I have a mixture of both and find that houses are easier to rent in certain areas – but flats also tend to be easier to rent in or near town or city centres.

WHERE WILL I FIND THE MONEY TO PAY FOR THE DEPOSIT?

1. BORROW FROM FAMILY

If you do not have savings that you can use as a deposit for your first purchase, there are other ways in which you can raise the capital. Probably the most common way is to borrow the money from family.

This is how I got started.

CASE STUDY: Borrowing from a family member
I sold a family member the idea of investing in buy-to-let property, and explained that I was prepared to offer them a 50/50 arrangement, whereby they would receive 50% of the rental income and 50% of the profit on the sale of the property. In return for lending me the money for my half of of the deposit

(the total deposit was 10% of the property value), I would pay 5% interest on that amount and take on full responsibility for managing the property and finances, and ensure they received a healthy profit once we decided to sell.

I did have to agree to sell this first property within a maximum of five years. As it happens, we ended up purchasing two houses within 12 months of each other, selling the first of them within two years. The first house we made a small profit of about £5,000 and the second we cleared a profit of £80,000 (£40,000 each). After that I was on my own and now had the capital to purchase more property.

When I purchased that first buy-to-let residential property in 1996 (this was my second property purchase) I only had one thought on my mind: buy at a reduced price and sell later for a big profit. At that time property prices were rising between 5 and 10% a year on average, and there seemed no end to year-on-year price increases. All I had to do was find enough cash to put down a 10% deposit and the rest was easy ... or so I thought.

Looking back now, what I experienced with that first buy-to-let property investment was invaluable. As explained earlier, I borrowed the £5,000 I needed for 50% of the deposit from a family member, and used £2,000 of my own money to pay for legal fees, stamp duty and all the other fees that need paying when purchasing a property. The house was on the market at £105,000 and I had negotiated a purchase price of £98,000. We put down a 10% deposit, leaving us with a mortgage of about £88,000 (after paying the 10% deposit) and monthly repayments of £600. I expected to get £750 a month for rental income, clearing a small rental profit for the year and then sit back and watch as the house increased in value over the next couple of years.

One small problem lay ahead that I hadn't accounted for. I couldn't let the property.

It remained empty for nine months at a cost of 9 × £600 (monthly mortgage payment), totalling £5,400. Eventually the letting agent did find a tenant who rented the house for six months at £750 a month, covering the mortgage payments for the rest of the time we owned the property.

Had I planned properly and ensured I had enough capital behind me to cover the first two years' mortgage payments, rather than assuming it would be easy to rent the property, I would have coped with these difficulties a lot better.

However, here's where my troubles really started. I had wanted to sell this property in the short term, making a healthy profit and enough to give me a deposit to purchase a larger four bedroom house (buy-to-let property number two), reaping even bigger profits in another year or two.

But I was stuck with a three-bedroom house that had now been on the market 15 months at £130,000, and it wasn't selling.

In the end the estate agent finally found us a buyer, and we ended up agreeing to sell the property for £120,000. After legal fees, estate agent fees, mortgage costs for 18 months (in total), and a kitchen extension, we ended up making a very small profit (between £4,000 and £5,000). Almost 20 years later I look back on the whole experience relieved we managed to make a small profit, taking into account how little planning and research I had conducted beforehand.

I carried on in the same vein for another few years; my aim was that all my buy-to-let purchases would produce great capital gain, and, as long as the rental income covered the monthly mortgage payments and expenses, I would be on course to profit. The property market did carry on booming, with prices rising on average at least 10% a year until the crash of 2007/2008.

During this period of growth, I only had one mission, and that was to keep borrowing, to keep buying, believing prices would keep rising. What happened in 2007/2008 put an end to that. I had to change my business entirely to survive. More on what I did in *Step 6: Developing Your Portfolio*.

> **TIP:** Finance
>
> Always make sure you have enough in the bank to cover you for any three months' void period. This might happen right after you purchase the property and need some time for repairs and maintenance work, or perhaps a year later when one lot of tenants move out and you have difficulty finding new tenants.

2. BORROW THE DEPOSIT FROM ELSEWHERE

Another option is to borrow the money for the deposit from the bank. With a good credit history and credit score, some banks are prepared to lend without any questions asked. Alternatively, you can apply for an overdraft facility, although you will need to check the interest rates you will be paying and add this extra cost into your calculations.

Six years after the 2007/2008 crash we are still feeling its effects. Banks in the US and the UK have been hoarding cash and are unwilling to lend. The good news is that things now seem to be getting better.

From 2008–2012 you needed a 25–40% deposit instead of the 10–20% that was acceptable before the crash. Interest rates on buy-to-let mortgages increased from 4% or 5% up to as much as 6–7%, affecting cash flow. These have since come back down to around 5–5.5%.

Fees on these mortgages also shot up. I had been paying on average £1,000 in one-time fees to the lender and this became an average of £2,000 from 2008 onwards. At the beginning of 2013, these fees started to come down somewhat too.

Interest rates, fees to the lender, loan to values, and mortgage products will always fluctuate and change depending on the economy and other outside factors, but it is important to be aware how much they can change when something like a recession comes along. You have to be prepared.

As I write, there are signs that the economy is picking up – albeit very slowly. If this continues, banks and building societies are going to become more competitive in the years ahead and getting loans should become easier. There will be more lenders offering mortgages with lower rates and lower fees. The loan to values will increase again and we won't need such large deposits.

Interest rates seem likely to stay low for quite some time; I predict they will stay below 2% up until the end of 2015. The government needs to stimulate the economy and raising interest rates is not going to help that. Because so many home owners are living in negative equity since the crash of 2007/08, and because so many people are and have been trying to pay back debt, the government knows it cannot increase interest rates without causing defaults. When they do eventually begin raising interest rates, they will have to do so very slowly. All this bodes well for property investors.

Low interest rates mean low borrowing costs, and a great advantage when borrowing from the banks is that you can fix the rate and the term.

> If you skipped or only skimmed *Step 2* because it was full of financial stuff, do go back and read the section on mortgages to make sure you understand what they're like in the buy-to-let world, and how to find the best ones.

3. RE-MORTGAGE YOUR OWN PROPERTY

You could re-mortgage the property you live in to raise the capital needed for an investment property. A simple explanation of this is laid out in the following example.

Example: re-mortgaging finance

Let's say the house you purchased to live in is currently worth £200,000 and you bought it for £120,000 so many years ago. You explain to your mortgage provider that you want to borrow £40,000 and that you believe the property to be worth £200,000. They will then value the property to ensure you have given them an accurate valuation. Once agreed on the value of your property, the bank will take into account that lending you this extra £40,000 means you would still have 20% equity in the house and their loan to value would equal 80%.

- **Your property valuation:** £200,000
- **Maximum loan:** 80% or £160,000
- **Your current mortgage:** £120,000

This would give you £40,000 to begin building your property portfolio. This would also still leave you with £40,000 equity in your property so even if property prices dropped by 10% you would still be in positive equity.

Now you need to work this into your calculations. You have borrowed an extra £40,000, which at 5% a year will cost you about £166 a month. Personally I would put aside £4,000 of this borrowed £40,000 to pay the interest for two years. This is where you have to be disciplined to ensure you do not spend this £4,000, but keep it just to cover the interest payments over the initial 24 months. Now you have £36,000 left to invest. How you use this £36,000 determines your future financial security.

This extra borrowing on your home is leverage, as covered in the previous step, and one of the most important and powerful things to learn when investing in property.

HOW MUCH WILL I NEED FOR A DEPOSIT AND OTHER COSTS?

There are other costs involved when purchasing an investment property and taking all of these costs into account is important. I have outlined here the basic costs involved:

A property investment purchased for £125,000

Cost of purchase	£125,000
Mortgage arrangement fee	£2,000
Solicitor costs (legal costs)	£1,000
Survey or valuation fee	£250
Home-buyer's report	£400
Stamp duty	£0 (for purchases up to £125,000)
Furnishing costs	£1,500
Redecoration costs	£700
One month's mortgage payment while looking for tenant	£500
One month's utility bills	£150
TOTAL purchase cost	£131,500

In 2002, I purchased two small two-bed terraced houses in the same street from the same vendor for £25,000 and £30,000, putting down 20% deposit on each property. I bought these properties at the same time as the vendor was looking to get rid of them as quick as possible and was therefore selling below market value. These two properties cost me £11,000 plus legal costs, decorative costs and furniture costs, bringing my total investment to about £15,000.

I remember thinking at the time, why don't more people do this? It seemed to make so much sense and having done my homework properly this time I could see that, even with an empty property for a few months, I was still going to make money. Having borrowed an extra £25,000 capital on our family home, which was costing me £100 a month, I had purchased two new houses with 80% mortgages, costing a total of about £300 a month, and I was earning more than £1,000 a month in rental income. This time I had prepared my finances properly. Having learnt from previous mistakes I needed to be absolutely sure I was taking everything into account.

I prepared a spreadsheet breaking down all my purchasing costs and a separate spreadsheet highlighting all my ongoing monthly costs:

Purchasing costs for two-bed house price at £25,000

1	Valuation/survey	£500
2	Deposit 20%	£5,000
3	Legal fees	£800
4	Stamp duty	£0
5	Mortgage fees	£400
6	Furniture	£1,000
	TOTAL purchase costs	**£7,700**

1. Valuation fee/survey: When you apply for a mortgage the mortgage provider or lender will survey and value the property to ensure the property is worth what it has been sold for, or thereabouts. The cost of this survey or valuation can vary depending on the lender. Some lenders will simply term this a valuation as they do not carry out a conclusive survey. Normally I will use an independent surveyor to carry out a home-buyer's report which will typically cost about £300–400. I have therefore calculated approximately £500 for both the survey and valuation.

2. Deposit: The amount of deposit can vary and again will depend on how much you want to put down or how much you can afford. The larger the deposit you put down, the better the mortgage terms.

3. Legal fees: Legal fees are made up of solicitor costs, local searches, and other government taxes. This amount can vary between £600 and £1,200.

4. Stamp duty: (SDLT) is charged on land and property transactions in the UK. The tax is charged at different rates and has different thresholds for different types of property and different values of transaction.

Residential land or property SDLT rates and thresholds

Purchase price/lease premium or transfer value	SDLT rate
Up to £125,000	Zero
Over £125,000 to £250,000	1%
Over £250,000 to £500,000	3%
Over £500,000 to £1 million	4%
£1 million to £2 million	5%

5. Mortgage fees: This is the amount the lender will charge you for arranging the mortgage. This can vary between 0.5–3% of the cost of the property.

6. Furniture: In most cases tenants are looking for furnished properties to rent. I normally allow between £1,500–2,000 depending on whether it is a two-bedroom or three-bedroom property.

Ongoing monthly costs

A	Mortgage payments	£130
B	Agent's management fee	£50
C	Buildings insurance	£20
D	Ground rent	£8 (£100 a year)
E	Maintenance	£20 (allowing £250 a year)
F	Council tax	£100
	Approximate monthly costs	£328

A. Mortgage payments: The monthly interest the lender charges you for the amount you have borrowed (on an interest only loan).

B. Agent's management fee: This is the amount the letting agent will charge you for managing the property, usually 5 to 10% + VAT.

C. Buildings insurance: You will need to take out buildings insurance on any freehold property you purchase. If it's a flat with a leasehold term agreement you will not require buildings insurance.

D. Ground rent: If you are purchasing a leasehold property then you will have to pay ground rent to the freeholder and service charges to the management company. It is very important to read the terms of the leasehold to find out how much the annual ground rent is and how much the monthly service charges will be.

E. Maintenance: You should always put aside a few hundred pounds for any maintenance jobs that might occur. I usually have a maintenance fund of £2,000 for urgent works that need carrying out.

F. Council tax: Council tax helps pay for local services like policing and rubbish collection. Council tax applies to all domestic properties, including houses, bungalows, flats, maisonettes, mobile homes and houseboats, whether owned or rented. Normally the tenant will pay the council tax. I do not pay any council tax on any of my buy-to-let properties and I ensure this is made clear on all my tenancy agreements.

Allowing for a few months when the property might be vacant, I calculated that with nine months rental income a year (three months empty), I would still be covered with an income of £4,500 less the above monthly costs. I tend to negotiate a fixed rate mortgage so I do not need to allow for interest rate fluctuations.

I had borrowed £25,000 and invested £15,000 in these two properties so intended to keep in reserve £10,000 in case of any emergency or problems I hadn't accounted for. The second property I purchased for £30,000, so the mortgage payments were a little higher, along with small increases to the monthly costs. However, carrying out the same due diligence and process as above, I calculated the figures and felt comfortable with the risks.

* * *

It's important to do the due diligence and attempt to work out your cash flow. By carrying out this process you can get an idea how the cash will flow into and out of your account, and whether the figures will work for you. It should also put your mind at rest before you take the leap and tie up all that money.

WHERE WILL I FIND GOOD TENANTS AND WHAT DO I NEED TO PREPARE FOR THEM?

If you do not have a full-time job and have the time to find your own tenants for your property, it will save you a few hundred pounds in agents fees and commission.

However, initially you might not have that free time or the wherewithal to find your own tenants. And that's not a problem.

I would recommend using a letting agent for the first one or two properties you purchase or until you are familiar with what's involved in finding tenants and renting out your property. There is a lot to consider and a letting agent will do all that initial work for you, albeit at a cost. A letting agent will find suitable tenants, obtain references, and prepare a tenancy agreement.

If your property is furnished they will also prepare an inventory of the contents. If you opt for the full management service then the agent will also collect the rent, organise the gas safety certificate, an EPC (Energy Performance Certificate), and pay the rent less their commission into your account every month. In certain cases, if I'm struggling to find the time, I will use the agents to find the tenants for me, prepare the tenancy agreement, and then take over the management of the property myself. Typical agents fees for managing property are 10% of the rent, but in most cases this will be negotiable. Typical agents fees for finding the tenants and preparing the agreement, as well as preparing the inventory are £450–550 + VAT. This is usually deducted from the first month's rent.

It is also the agent's responsibility to take up references for potential tenants from previous landlords, employers and so on, to help ensure the rent will be met and that the tenants are of good character.

Finding a good, reputable agent is important. I suggest asking any other local landlord for a recommendation. If you do not know any local landlords then I recommend visiting some of the agents and talking to them. Have a list of questions you want to ask them and gauge how they deal with your queries. You can obtain quite a lot of information and get a good feel for the agent by asking relevant questions. You should also ask them if they are a member of one of the recognised professional bodies, such as the OEA – Ombudsman for Estate Agents. This will give you peace of mind, and should guarantee a reasonable standard of competence. Questions you should ask the agent will be covered in *Step 5: Managing Your portfolio – Renting and Letting*.

FINDING TENANTS YOURSELF

If you decide to find tenants without using an agent then there are various ways of doing so. You could advertise in the local paper or local shop windows for a low cost. There are many websites for finding tenants, some free and some at a cost. Gumtree (**www.gumtree.co.uk**) is probably the most used website for advertising for tenants; it is easy to use and inexpensive. Other good websites include **www.houseladder.co.uk, www.zoopla.co.uk**.

Take photos of your property inside and out. Make sure you use a good quality camera and take photos during the day when it is light outside. The more photos, the better. Write a well-written description of the property: you want to attract good reliable tenants, such as young professionals with reliable incomes, so you need to appeal to them with a professionally put-together advert for your property.

Just because there are websites you can advertise on for free, do not discount paying for ads too. You are trying to find high quality tenants, so do not discount paying to advertise on other websites, where young professional people might be looking, such as **www.landlordlet.com**.

It is important to check references, even if you meet your potential tenants and like them. Even if you are a good judge of character, you should do all you can to ensure they are genuine. Unfortunately, there are some rogue tenants out there who will happily take on a six-month tenancy, pay the deposit and first month's rent and then pay nothing else. After a couple of months, the landlord will begin court proceedings in order to repossess the property and obtain rent arrears, only for the tenant to disappear before the court order is made. This then leaves the landlord with four or five months of unpaid rent, court proceedings costs and in some cases damage to the property.

I would strongly recommend asking your tenant for bank account details and ask them to sign a standing order mandate paying the rent into your account the same date each month for the duration of the agreement.

By getting them to sign a standing order mandate, they are making some kind of initial commitment, and it saves you the hassle and bother of having to meet each month to collect the rent.

There is no guarantee that you will end up with the ideal tenants even after taking all the necessary precautions, but you are more likely to have fewer problematic tenants if you take out and check the references before agreeing to rent out your property. If a tenant is renting for the first time then they will not be able to provide any references from previous landlords, so it's important to also request a reference from their current employer. If they can do this then you know they are employed and have an income with which to pay the rent.

If you decide to rent to students or someone who is unemployed, I would recommend asking the tenant for a surety or guarantor, who is then responsible for paying the rent if the tenant fails to do so.

Personally, I try to avoid renting to students. Students tend to rent for nine to ten months (term time), hold lots of parties which can upset the neighbours, and tend to be less careful with your property than young professionals or young families. I am generalising, of course, but in my experience I have found my properties to be kept in better condition by young professionals or young families than by students.

You can stipulate that tenants sign a 12-month tenancy agreement and pay for the full 12 months, but in every case where I have rented to students they have left my property after the 12 months in need of a complete refurbishment. When I use a letting agent to find tenants I now ask them to try to find young families who they feel might stay for a couple of years or more. I once rented a house to four young students who left the property in a poor state with badly stained carpets, big holes in the walls where they had hung pictures, and damaged furniture. They also decided to take half of the small furnishings with them. They disappeared before the end of the tenancy. Fortunately they had paid a £1,200 deposit and I insisted on using all of this towards the property being refurbished and replacing the stolen furniture.

There are advantages and disadvantages to renting and letting yourself, and you will need to decide whether to manage your first few properties or to give them to a letting agent to manage.

In *Step 5: Managing Your Portfolio* I have written further about renting and letting and what is involved in finding reliable tenants and managing your portfolio.

SUMMING UP

Purchasing your first investment property can be quite daunting when you haven't had the experience before. That's why it's so important to do plenty of research, use the services and help of estate agents, mortgage brokers, other landlords and letting agents to guide you through your first purchase. Finding a good mortgage broker and getting to know all the local estate agents and letting agents will play an important part in building your team, the subject of the next step. The more help you can get in the early stages of developing your portfolio, the more likely you are to make fewer mistakes.

STEP 4.

BUILDING YOUR TEAM

INTRODUCTION

WITH ANY BUSINESS there is only so much you can do on your own. I recommend getting to know as many people as possible who can help you in the early stages of becoming a property investor and property landlord. The great thing with property is that there are many people you can count on as part of your team, including mentors, likeminded people you meet at local property networking groups, builders and tradesmen, local estate agents and letting agents.

MENTORS

Property can be a very lonely business, especially in the earlier years if you are trying to do everything yourself. Many property investors I know went in search of a mentor to help them in the earlier stages of their development and I was no different.

Earlier in the book I mentioned I had two mentors, one a family member who had a lot of experience running his own businesses, and who was never afraid to go it alone, and a second mentor who had been in the property business for more than 20 years when we first became acquainted. This second mentor, who was very important to me in the early years, felt like part of my team.

Whatever business you choose to go into on your own, it's important to try and surround yourself with people who can help you, whether it be a mentor or a partner or just a friend. We all need guidance and support when we are starting out, so to have a team of people around us – even if it's just someone to talk to and bounce ideas off – is paramount.

NETWORKING

Check out your local area for free seminars and workshops. I joined a local property networking group who meet the last Monday of every month and invite experts and experienced investors to talk about where they are up to in their business and to discuss current topics. The cost to join is a mere £10 a month. Each month a panel of experts in their field will update the members with the latest information regarding mortgages, tax, legal issues and anything relevant to property investors and the buy-to-let market.

This is vital to building your own business. These meetings are regularly attended by small part-time investors, long-time experienced investors and others who might only be interested and attending to get a taste for property. Usually there will be a guest speaker who in some cases will be inspirational and motivating, and perhaps other times less so. However, in every meeting I have attended I have come away feeling I had gleaned some important information or learnt something new relating to property investment.

In the early stages of building your portfolio, the people you meet and network with at these meetings can also become a part of your team as they did for me. The more people you talk to and meet who have the same passion and interest in property as you do, the more it helps to make those first couple of years feel less lonely. The key is to talk to and get to know as many likeminded people as you can. Some of those I have met in the past have given me valuable advice and tips and recommended tradesmen, mortgage brokers, financial advisers, accountants and so on.

There is, however, only so much you can learn at these seminars, workshops and meetings. You will need to go out there and take action at some point, and in order to do this it is important you find yourself a good mentor, someone who has seen it all, done it, been there and can give you all the guidance and help you need to get going.

My property mentor was a good friend and had been buying and selling property for more than 20 years. This mentor had at one time built up a portfolio of more than 100 properties. I felt he might be able to teach me a thing or two. To begin with, he was able to put me in contact with a mortgage broker who organised my first buy-to-let mortgage and buildings insurance. Although I only used his services twice he was a part of my team when I started out on my new venture.

My mentor guided me, pointed me in the right direction and gave me lots of good advice, but as all good mentors should do, he began loosening the reins after a few months and wanted me to find my own team, find my own way, do my own homework and research and build as many contacts as possible.

BUILDERS AND TRADESMEN

Within your team should be someone who is going to manage and carry out most of your property repairs and maintenance work. This person, for me, is one of the most important people in the team. This person needs to be someone you can trust, someone you know isn't pulling the wool over your eyes, and at the same time is a good, reputable, professional tradesman.

This particular member of your team does not necessarily have to be a qualified plumber, electrician, builder, plasterer and so on, but he needs to be reputable, experienced, trustworthy and know the appropriate tradesmen who do belong to a trade body for their profession.

Over the years I have amassed a great team of plumbers, electricians, plasterers, kitchen-fitters, bedroom furniture fitters and so on. All of these tradesman can be individuals running their own businesses, but who all know each other through years of working on the same jobs together.

In the case of a house I purchased in 2006 that needed a complete overhaul, I employed six or seven different tradesman who had all worked together in the past, all knew each other and were able to liaise with each other to ensure the jobs were carried out in the right order and in time to meet the deadline. You will need one person or tradesman to manage and oversee any big jobs such as a complete house renovation, someone you can trust to knit it all together and to speak with all the different individuals to ensure the job runs smoothly.

Of course, if you have time you can save money by carrying out your own maintenance and repair work. I would only recommend this scenario if you have had plenty of experience doing DIY jobs and have the correct tools to do so. My property mentor preferred to carry out as much repair work as he possibly could in his early years as a landlord. Once his portfolio grew and he became too busy for this, he employed someone to carry out the work for him.

Once you have a good team of reliable workmen working for you it makes running your portfolio a whole lot easier, but you have to start somewhere. I didn't have one good contact when I started out with my first buy-to-let property. If you find yourself in a similar situation I would strongly recommend that you speak to everyone you know who owns property, and ask for recommendations (or warnings).

Whenever you choose a building company or an individual tradesman, it is important to check them out and make sure they are a member of a trade body for their profession. Find out how long they have been in business and whether they have the necessary liability insurance. I would ask for references for previous work they have carried out and call those references to ask for feedback. I always ask for at least two references and ask as many questions of those references as possible, such as: how good the quality of workmanship was, whether they completed the job when they said they would, whether they charged what they quoted, if they were clean and tidy in their work and so on.

TIP: Finding tradesmen

If you are struggling to find recommended tradesmen, go to the local bathroom showroom, local DIY store, and local tile shop and ask if they can recommend a good plumber or electrician. Most independent plumbers and electricians will frequent these stores on a regular basis and word gets around.

In the early years of building your portfolio, and when you haven't yet built an established team of tradesman, it is important to get a variety of quotes for all jobs that need attending to. You can of course go too far and have too many quotes, but I would recommend two or three quotes for smaller jobs such as plumbing, fitting a new boiler, or electric work such as a re-wiring job, and three to five quotes for bigger jobs such as a full renovation.

When we had our family home renovated, which involved seven months work and a double storey extension, we had five lots of quotes, two of which were established building firms recommended to us by the architect who drew up the plans, and three of them from smaller businesses who worked on their own and subcontracted certain jobs to other tradesman.

We wanted to go with one of the larger building firms who had come recommended by the architect and who impressed us when we met. He was very professional and we felt we could trust his team to carry out a good job. However, the two larger firms quoted us almost double the price quoted to us by the three smaller businesses. The reason being that the larger firms have larger overheads.

I also gathered later that both these businesses had a full book of jobs and quoted on the high side as they would have had to bring in more tradesman to cater for our job if we chose to go with them. Of the other three quotes we received, all of which were within £5,000 of each other, we decided to opt for the one we felt most comfortable with. This might not be your preferred way of choosing who to employ for the job, but I have nearly always found that going with my gut feeling has stood me in good stead.

And so this proved the case with this job, we were really pleased with the end result, really happy with the quality of the workmanship, and very happy to recommend this builder to friends and family in the future. In fact, we did and believe he has carried out at least three further jobs as a result of our recommendations.

It's not always a good idea to go with the cheapest quote you receive; it's more important that you go with your gut feeling and equally as important that you get on with the builder and are able to establish a rapport with them.

CONTRACT – AGREEMENT

Always agree a timescale with your builder, get everything in writing and ensure you have a thorough agreement drawn up for any big jobs, such as a house extension or full renovation. I wouldn't go as far as recommending having a legal contract drawn up, as many builders are not happy taking on jobs where there's too much legal jargon to contend with.

I have found from experience, and from talking with other investors, that a legally drawn up agreement brings it's own problems. In nearly all cases where there is a big job being carried out, there are certain issues or problems that will arise during the job, and very often these are better ironed out face to face, and amicably, with your builder. Because these small issues or problems will nearly always arise during a long-term project, many builders will want to avoid any complex legal agreement.

On the other hand, if you do not trust the builder you have appointed and do not feel you want to take any chances, then you might prefer to seek legal advice as to whether you should have a contract drawn up. You will need to check with your builder that they are prepared to sign this agreement.

PLANNING PERMISSION AND BUILDING REGULATIONS

You may also need to apply for planning permission and obtain building regulations approval. If you appoint an architect they can handle the process for you. A good architect will be able to give you good advice and tell you what they believe will be acceptable to the planning department before applying. A typical extension should be dealt with within six to eight weeks and will depend on your local office (some are quicker than others). The work should adhere to building regulations and an officer will come out to inspect the job and ensure all guidelines have been properly adhered to.

* * *

Once you have established your team of builders and tradesman it is important to stay in touch with them and let them know you will want to use their services again in the future. When you have found a good reputable plumber and electrician they can play a very valuable role in helping to maintain your portfolio.

I have often had to text my plumber while working away, or on holiday, and ask him to visit one of my properties in the case of a burst pipe or faulty boiler. Knowing he will take care of the job for me as soon as possible and that I can trust him to do the job quickly and efficiently without ripping me off gives me peace of mind when I am away. The plumber, on the other hand, knows I will pay him for the job as soon as I return, and that he will continue to get all the work for all my properties in the future for looking after me.

ESTATE AGENTS / LETTING AGENTS

It also helps if you can include estate agents as part of your team, and by that I mean that you will be the first person they think of when there is a good deal to be had. Years ago I was determined to buy a particular property and found myself in a real tussle with some other parties who were also interested in the same property. This property was a real find and had a lot of potential.

I had negotiated a good price and was really pleased with myself. However, weeks before completing on the purchase, two other interested parties appeared on the scene and offered a higher price than we had already agreed. Normally I would expect the vendor to stick with the agreed sale, especially when much of the legal work had already been completed.

However, one of the new interested parties was offering £5,000 more than I had, and appeared to be a legitimate buyer. Because I had built up a good relationship with the sales manager, I felt I could ask specific questions to gain as much information as I could about the vendor and the new interested party. I felt the agent was on my side because he was feeding me information that I wasn't expecting him to.

I explained to him at this juncture that I really wanted this property, that I had a good track record with his company, and was so close to completion that it wasn't in anyone's interest to consider other offers.

He ensured the deal went through.

I believe the agent acted in good faith on behalf of the vendor. He could have tried to get a higher offer from me, or perhaps could have persuaded the vendor to consider the higher offer from the other party, but there was always the possibility that the sale would have fallen through and the agent and vendor would have had to have started the sale process all over again. In my mind the sales manager was ensuring the sale went through with a reputable buyer. I have found that by keeping in regular contact with certain agents, and always being as friendly (whilst remaining serious and professional) as possible, you can count some of these agents as part of your team.

SUMMING UP

Building your team and having good reputable professional people working for you is a massive help in ensuring your business runs smoothly. Remember that good professional work carried out on your property will enhance the overall appearance and add to the value of that property.

STEP 5.

MANAGING YOUR PORTFOLIO

INTRODUCTION

YOU CAN CHOOSE to manage your own properties or decide to let an agent manage them for you. This decision really comes down to whether you have time to manage them yourself, and whether you *want* to manage them yourself.

There are advantages and disadvantages in both cases; this chapter will cover these points in order to help you decide.

Should you decide to give your properties to a letting agent or management company to manage, there are certain important questions to ask beforehand and certain tasks that you will need to carry out. If you do decide to manage your own properties than you will need to know how to go about renting your property, where to advertise, how to prepare a tenancy agreement, what laws you need to adhere to regarding gas and electricity safety, how to obtain buildings insurance, and you will need to know what to do if you want to get rid of troublesome tenants. All of this is covered in this chapter.

THE ADVANTAGES OF MANAGING YOUR OWN PROPERTIES

1. LEARNING THE BUSINESS

In the early years of getting your property empire off the ground, managing your own properties can hep you learn the business – it gives you an education in all of the ins and outs of property letting (actually crucial for delegating more effectively later on, if you want to).

The best way to do this is to actually have an agent manage your first buy-to-let property for you so that you can see firsthand how to prepare your property for rent and what paperwork needs taking care of. You need to learn the business, have the skills and know-how to find and manage tenants, prepare short-hold tenancy agreements, collect rent, deal with problematic tenants, respond to any issues with repairs and renewals and so on. Working with an agent will give you all this in pretty short order if you make it your mission to find out as much of this information as possible from them during your first buy-to-let investment. It will leave you in a much better position to manage buy-to-let property numbers two, three and four.

2. SAVING MONEY

Another reason to manage your own property is to save you money.

Typical management fees are 10–12.5% of the property's rent, which can amount to quite a lot over 12 months. If you own three houses, bringing in a total of £30,000 rent a year, then you are giving away £3,000 of that to the managing agent – plus finders' fee costs (finding new tenants).

In the earlier years of building your portfolio this £3,000 + fees could be put towards a deposit on your next property investment.

You can try to negotiate with a letting agent, and if you are offering them more than one property to manage certain agents will agree a discount. In the past I have negotiated a 7% management fee for three properties, and more recently 6% for the management of six or more properties.

3. MAKING GOOD CONTACTS

In the first few years of building your portfolio you can get to know the local tradesmen that the agent or management company uses for repairs and maintenance. If you ask for copies of all legal documents, tenancy agreements and letters they send on your behalf you will have some valuable information at your finger-tips without having to do the legwork yourself.

THE DISADVANTAGES OF MANAGING YOUR OWN PROPERTIES

There are a few disadvantages of self managing although some of them only apply in the early stages of your buy-to-let business.

1. LACK OF EXPERIENCE AND EXPERTISE

If you are starting out and you decide to go it alone to save money, without the experience and knowledge it can be quite a steep and expensive learning curve. If you don't have good contacts, for example, you may decide to try and do some repair work yourself, only creating more long-term damage and ending up with a more costly repair bill.

And without the experience in dealing with tenants, you may end up with all sorts of problems – including late payments, a dispute over the deposit or even some legal issue – and not know how to deal with them in the appropriate manner.

2. STRESS

Having to be on call at all times can be quite stressful, especially if tenants are calling regularly and there are lots of teething problems at the beginning of a tenancy. This can then lead to even bigger problems if the issues aren't dealt with quickly and efficiently. Even when on holiday, it can be difficult to relax knowing a tenant could call at any time.

3. TIME

There are so many things to consider and jobs to be carried out when managing your own property and this can be very time-consuming. There is a lot of paperwork involved, much of it a legal requirement. An agent will organise the gas safety certificate for you and the Energy Performance Certificate (EPC). Since 2008 all rental properties have to have one of these. The cost is about £60–80 and you can choose your own energy assessor at **www.epcregister.com**.

My recommendation is to start out managing your own properties – albeit after following an agent managing your very first one. Then, after a few years and once your portfolio has grown beyond three or four properties, it usually makes sense to start handing over the reins.

Once you have decided whether to manage your own property or let an agent manage it for you, you then need to decide whether to rent your property through an agent or to try and rent it yourself. Most established agents will have a 'letting-only service' or a 'letting and management service'.

THE ADVANTAGES OF LETTING THROUGH AN AGENT

1. THEY HAVE THE KNOWLEDGE AND EXPERTISE

Letting is an agent's area of expertise. A good agent will know what rental value you can expect for your property and give you good advice on how to prepare your property for the right market. Listen and learn so you know what you are doing should you decide to go it alone in the future.

2. THEY WILL TAKE CARE OF THE FINANCES

An agent will collect the first month's rent and take care of the deposit, registering it with the TDS (Tenancy Deposit Scheme), now a legal requirement. They should also get the tenant to set up a standing order mandate so that the rent automatically gets paid into the agent's account every month.

3. MARKETING

The toughest part of renting out your property is finding good, reliable tenants. A good agent should be able to find you tenants quickly and deal with the paperwork and tenancy agreement in a matter of days.

If you choose to give your property to an agent or management company, it is advisable to make sure that they are a member of the National Approved Letting Scheme, a member of ARLA (the Association of Residential Letting Agents), or the UK Association of Letting Agents. Ask for a concise breakdown of all their fees, including VAT, before signing any agreements. Most agents will want to charge you a fee for renewing a tenancy agreement if your existing tenants want to stay for another year. You can usually negotiate this with the agent and either agree no renewal fee if the same tenant renews, or a 50% reduction in the renewal fee.

4. YOU WILL HAVE MORE TIME TO THINK ABOUT BUILDING YOUR PORTFOLIO

If you are spending most of your time looking after your existing portfolio, you will not leave yourself enough time to develop the portfolio further. There does come a point when you will feel you are spending most of your time attending to small problems or issues with tenants and needless paperwork. It's at this point that you should let the experts do what they do best in order to free up your time to do what you do best.

CASE STUDY: Agent handover

I reached the point when it made sense to hand over managing my properties to a letting agent at ten properties. I had held off for as long as possible because I wanted to keep as much profit from the rental income as possible to re-invest it in building my portfolio. But I found myself thinking and focusing on the smaller issues most of the day and I realised that I would be better off paying an agent to manage the portfolio so that I could spend more time focusing on developing the portfolio further. Certainly, by the time you get to ten properties, you should be in a strong enough position financially to bring in someone to manage your properties.

DISADVANTAGES OF LETTING THROUGH AN AGENT

1. IT CAN BE COSTLY

An agent will normally charge a hefty fee for finding a tenant and drawing up the tenancy agreement and dealing with the paperwork. Fees vary, but I normally get charged about £500 + VAT. On top of this, the agent will also charge the tenant a fee.

Even if you decide to take over managing the property once the tenant is signed up, the agent will still look to benefit from renewing the agreement once it expires. I always make it clear to the agent that I will be drawing up my own tenancy agreement with the tenants should they decide to renew for another period. This not only saves you another £500 + VAT, but also saves the tenant a renewal fee.

2. YOUR PROPERTY WILL BE LET UNDER THE AGENCY'S TERMS, NOT YOURS

If you let through an agent, always read the contract thoroughly. They might have a three months' notice to cancel the agreement, where you only want a one month's notice. If the agent is managing the property for you, read the contract carefully to determine what the agent will deal with; for example, chasing arrears and handling repairs for you.

If you decide to let your property through an agent there are certain questions you could or should ask them. There are many good letting agents in the UK who are members of trade bodies, which offer some kind of regulation, but there are even more agents who are not regulated – which can bring about problems further down the road.

Important questions to ask a letting agent

- How long does it currently take from advertising to finding a tenant?

- Have you anyone on your books currently looking for my type of property?

- What are your fees for finding tenants?

- What are your ongoing fees for managing and maintaining my property?

- Can you provide me a written copy of all your fees?

- How many properties similar to mine are you marketing?

- Where will you be advertising my property?

- Will you put a picture and description in your window?

- What websites do you advertise on?

- Arc you a member of a trade body?

- Can I see a copy of the tenancy agreement you get the tenants to sign? (You should ask to take a copy away with you to read as this will undoubtedly throw up some further questions.)

- What happens if the tenant leaves before the end of the tenancy?

- What happens if the tenant misses a payment?

- What is the process for getting rid of bad tenants?

- What checks do you carry out on the tenants?

- What is the process for checking out tenants at the end of the tenancy?

It is important to keep everything in a filing system. Invest in a filing cabinet and aim to fill it. I purchased a lovely wooden four door cabinet which took me ten years to fill; I now have a second one that is almost full so will be ordering a third very shortly. Never throw any paperwork away. Keep all receipts, invoices, statements, tenancy agreements, legal documents and anything relating to your portfolio. You will need all of this information for your end-of-year accounts, and if you want to manage your portfolio efficiently. HMRC will want to see your last six years' paperwork if it decides to look into your affairs.

HMOs

As part of your strategy you will also need to decide whether you want to rent to young professionals, students, married couples, tenants with pets or without pets and so on.

Do you want to rent your property under a single let agreement, or as an HMO (house of multiple occupancy)? A house of multiple occupancy is a property rented out to a group of people, each having their own tenancy agreement, as they do not know each other or are not related.

The definition of an HMO is a property occupied by more than one household, who share amenities such as a bathroom, toilet or cooking facilities.

At the moment, in England and Wales, landlords with HMOs of three storeys or more and with five or more tenants have to get a licence. The licence will specify the maximum number of people who may live in the HMO. It will also include conditions concerning gas safety certificates, electrical appliances and furniture, smoke alarms and tenancy agreements (each occupier must have a written tenancy agreement).

The local council has the power to refuse a licence if your property does not meet certain standards. Penalties for not getting a licence are quite severe. These licences impose tough management standards which in turn impose extra costs to ensure that properties comply with safety standards and are not occupied by too many people.

Having an HMO means being able to let your property to more tenants, and therefore generating extra rental income, but more tenants means more regulations. If you rent to five or more people each bedroom has to have a washbasin. The rules and regulations for HMOs are constantly under review and constantly being opposed by landlords wanting to apply for HMOs, so I recommend looking into this in greater detail as by the time you read this the laws might have changed again.

One of the disadvantages of owning HMOs is that of time management and cost. Some of the questions I asked myself when considering them were:

- Do I have the time to manage each bedroom as a separate let and manage each tenant as an individual agreement?
- How much will it cost to install washbasins in each bedroom and adhere to the extra fire and safety regulations?
- What if one tenant in one room is upsetting the tenants in the other rooms?
- What extra cost will be incurred as each tenant vacates, and I need to get the rooms renovated on a room-by-room basis?

Some lenders are not comfortable with HMOs and restrict amounts they're willing to lend towards establishing them. This can determine how much interest you end up paying and affect your cash flow. I know some landlords who recently sold up due to the increase in costs and compliance laws.

I have looked into HMOs on many occasions and know some landlords who make a good living from running HMO properties. However, this is a full-time job and requires a lot of time and money to make it work. Personally, I prefer a single let with a 12-month tenancy agreement, where I do not need to make lots of internal alterations to the property and manage each room as a separate agreement. I believe in the long run that, though I am not receiving as much rental income, my costs are a lot lower and the time and commitment involved is a lot less.

INSURANCE

Before purchasing a property, you will need to get it insured, unless it's a flat with a leasehold agreement, in which case the insurance will nearly always be covered by the freeholder. Certain city centre apartments I purchased are on 250-years leasehold agreements. When I first purchased these apartments I didn't know that this was the case and contacted a well-known insurance provider to insure the properties. At no time did they ask me if the property was a leasehold or freehold property. When I finally realised that the apartments were already insured through the freeholder's insurance, some two years later, I contacted the insurance company who duly refunded the buildings insurance I had paid during those two years.

If you wish to insure any contents such as furniture then you need to take out separate contents insurance. I always explain to my tenants that they should consider taking out their own contents insurance for valuables such as laptops, computers, TVs, and any jewellery they might own.

Some buy-to-let mortgage companies and landlords associations have specialist buildings insurance policies for landlords. You can also obtain landlords insurance through commercial insurance brokers. Most policies will include a small amount of contents cover which should be enough to cover the basics and any furniture you might provide. Cover for loss of rent should be provided too.

Most policies will include cover for public and employer's liability up to £5m. Also check that there is a 24-hour emergency call out feature on the policy, as the insurer will send out their emergency tradesmen to fix any problem with the cost covered. If you take out separate emergency cover this can be quite costly. Check the details with your insurer and ask how much the emergency cover is. Always check the policy exclusions. Some policies won't cover short-term lets or tenants on housing benefit. Most policies won't cover properties that have been left empty for more than three weeks unless the insurer has been notified in advance.

All policies are different, so it is important that you read them carefully to see what is covered and what isn't.

RENTING YOURSELF

Apart from getting insurance cover, there's a good deal of work involved in ensuring your property is ready for renting. Just before letting you will need to take meter readings for gas, electricity and water and notify the utility suppliers.

When you call them with the readings you can give them the tenant's contact details and the start date of the tenancy agreement at the same time. Give the meter readings to your tenants and inform them that you have given the same readings to the utility companies.

Some landlords keep the council tax in their name, and take the amount into consideration when setting the monthly rent amount. I prefer to notify the council of the new tenant's names and make them liable for the council tax. It avoids making you look like you're overcharging compared to other properties which don't include the council tax. A two-bedroom flat renting for £550 a month could become £650 a month if it includes council tax. Though this isn't any more expensive than renting and having to pay council tax separately, the top line amount deters potential tenants.

GAS

You need to ensure that all gas appliances are maintained and in good order and that an annual safety check is carried out by a gas-safe registered installer. Provided everything is OK, the engineer will provide you with a landlord's gas safety certificate. You will need to obtain this gas safety certificate every 12 months. It is also strongly advisable to install carbon monoxide detectors.

ELECTRICITY

Whilst there is no legal requirement to have annual safety checks on electrical equipment, you do need to ensure all electrical appliances are checked and comply with safety standards. I use a qualified electrician to carry out these checks on all the appliances before new tenants move in and then provide them with instruction manuals for each appliance.

FIRE SAFETY

Any furniture you provide must comply with the Furniture and Furnishings (Fire) (Safety) Regulations 1998. If you are purchasing new furniture for any of your properties, make sure it has the manufacturer's label on it saying it meets these requirements.

You should also provide a mains-operated smoke alarm on each level of the property. At the very least you should also provide battery-operated smoke alarms for you and your tenants' peace of mind. I always check that these are working before the tenants move in and ask them to check them regularly and replace the batteries when needed.

* * *

Once all these checks are in place, your property is almost ready to rent. Now you need to prepare your property for viewings. Once all the furniture is in place and all the safety procedures have been carried out, I get the property cleaned and carry out a thorough inspection to ensure everything is in good working order.

Make sure the garden is tidy and everything cut back. If there is a garden, the tenancy agreement should stipulate that the tenants are responsible for the upkeep. You should point out to the tenants that the garden has just been tended to and tidied and that it's their responsibility to ensure it is in the same or similar condition at the end of the tenancy.

You should try to keep your spending and costs as low as possible, so avoid buying expensive furniture and fittings. Try to buy things that are hardwearing so you don't have to replace them every year. Make your property bright and airy using light-coloured curtains or fabrics.

I would recommend buying good quality mattresses. If you buy cheap, poor quality beds and mattresses your tenants will soon ask you to replace them.

Curtains should be machine-washable. If you don't want to buy curtains, install roller-blinds or muslin fabrics. Some agents and landlords will tell you to avoid light-coloured carpets as they show up marks and stains, but I recommend light-coloured carpets with a fleck design as these make the rooms look bigger and feel brighter. If you are concerned about providing carpets and then having to replace them every year due to heavy wear and tear, hardwood or laminate flooring is a good alternative. I like to have laminate flooring in the hallway and provide a rug to create a sense of warmth. Hardwood or laminate flooring in a flat can cause a problem if your tenants have young kids that run around a lot. You will most likely receive calls of complaint from the people living below your flat.

Try to stick to the same, bright-coloured paint for all your properties. I use white or magnolia because they brighten the property and are the least expensive.

Windows should be cleaned inside and out. The appropriate bins should be provided and listed in the inventory list. All kitchen cupboards and appliances (fridge freezer, washing machine etc.) should be clean. Weather permitting, air the property for a few days before you start showing tenants around, so there is no damp or lingering smells. Ensure you have keys for all the doors and windows.

CONDENSATION AND DAMP

Condensation and damp can be very problematic. Most new-build properties include extractor fans and air vents. But most properties are not new-builds.

A landlord cannot expect tenants to ventilate a property if they have not been provided with adequate ventilation. I always make a point of asking my tenants to keep windows open in the bathroom when using the shower or bath, though this is an unreasonable request during the winter. I have often had mould issues in properties without adequate ventilation and now try to ensure that I provide the necessary ventilation. Tenants are responsible for cleaning mouldy surfaces but residual staining would be considered fair wear and tear.

GO THE EXTRA MILE

I like to go the extra mile and ensure my properties look attractive and have a homely feel. For a small cost, you can provide flowers for the kitchen, soaps and bath foam for the bathrooms, towels and bath and toilet mats. I cover the mattresses with sheets or a blanket and any older scuffed furniture with a throw or blanket. I buy a few scented candles for the living room and put paintings or pictures in each room. Some landlords might feel this is going a bit too far, but a clean, tidy and homely looking property is going to make a much greater impact than something that looks tired and run down. The tenants feel they are renting from a good, reliable landlord who cares about his tenants. It assures them that they will be looked after if any problems arise. I also welcome my tenants with a bottle of wine and some chocolates, as I believe the more you treat your tenants with respect and warmth, the more likely they are to treat your property the same way.

By going that extra mile and making your property attractive for prospective tenants, you will never have any problem letting your property. Word of mouth is a powerful thing, and before you know it you will be getting calls regularly from friends of your tenants looking for property to rent. Years ago I started renting to some tenants from the Czech Republic; before long I had numerous properties rented to Czech people, friends of those first tenants who had recommended me as a good, professional landlord who had clean, tidy and well-managed properties.

About four or five years ago I rented a three-bed property to some Polish tenants who in turn recommended me to Polish friends of theirs. I now have 12 properties let to Polish people, all without having to advertise or use an agent to find tenants. I receive regular calls from friends of friends of existing tenants looking for property to rent and have to turn most of them away. It really doesn't take long to build up a good reputation in an area if you look after your tenants and ensure your properties are in good condition.

TENANCY AGREEMENTS

ASSURED SHORT-HOLD TENANCY

The assured short-hold tenancy is the most common form of tenancy. Most tenancy agreements are automatically this type. Assured short-hold tenancies apply when:

- the property is privately owned by the landlord.
- the landlord isn't living in the property.
- the tenants living in your property treat the property as their main accommodation.

A short-hold tenancy cannot apply if:

- it's a business tenancy or a tenancy of licenced premises
- it's a holiday let
- the rent is more than £100,000 a year
- the rent is less than £250 a year
- your landlord is a local council.

EXCLUDED TENANCY OR LICENCE

An excluded tenancy or licence may apply if a tenant is living with a landlord and sharing a bathroom or kitchen. Normally a tenant will have less protection from eviction in this case.

GET AN AGREEMENT IN PLACE!

It's important to have a legal agreement in place when letting to tenants. You are leaving yourself open to all sorts of possible problems and potential conflict with bad tenants if a tenancy agreement isn't in place from the outset.

The point of having an agreement in place is to clearly define the obligations and responsibilities between the landlord and the tenant. There are many places one can obtain a standard tenancy agreement that can be used for renting houses or flats. Check out:

- www.tenancyagreementservice.co.uk
- www.rla.org.uk
- www.lawdepot.co.uk

An assured short-hold tenancy is normally for a fixed period of six to 12 months. At the end of this term the landlord can take back the property or agree to draw up a new contract if both parties want to continue with the arrangement.

If the landlord decides to take back the property at the end of the agreement two months' notice have to be given. I prefer to start with a six-month contract so I can see how things work out and whether the tenants make payments on time. If all goes well and they are happy to stay beyond the six months I will then consider a 12-month renewal on the agreement.

Once drawn up, ensure the agreement is signed by you, as landlord, the tenant and an independent witness. If you are using an agent they will have their own standard contract but as mentioned earlier, ensure you read this carefully as you may want them to add in certain clauses.

For example; should you agree to rent to tenants with pets, you might want the agent to add a clause whereby the tenant has to 'make good' any damage caused by their pets before vacating the property. I once agreed to rent to tenants with two dogs on the condition they paid two months' deposit to cover any potential damage. If you are providing the agreement rather than the agent, make two copies, one for you and one for the tenant, ensuring both are signed by all parties. When signing the agreement I ask for the deposit and first month's rent – i.e. before the tenant moves into the property.

If there is more than one tenant signing the agreement then each person is jointly liable for the full rent. If three tenants are renting a property from you, paying a total of £900, and one tenant decides to vacate the property early, the other two tenants are then liable for that person's share of £300. I recently had a situation where one tenant moved out of one of my properties so the other two decided to give me notice to vacate the property as they couldn't afford to pay the extra rent. Thankfully they found a friend at short notice to fill the third room, saving me the hassle of having to re-let the property. All I had to do was prepare a new agreement replacing one name for another under the same terms.

GETTING RID OF BAD TENANTS

As soon as a tenant misses a payment, unfortunately it's vital to take the appropriate action. Sadly, being too soft will generally leave you open to further problems and further missed payments. It's actually better for everyone's sake that things are dealt with quickly and cleanly.

No landlord ever wants to fall out with their tenants. They want to build longstanding relationships. But you have to treat your property portfolio as a business. The process of eviction is never easy and can take *months*, so it's important to act swiftly to avoid a hefty financial burden building up.

When a tenant misses a payment, most inexperienced landlords listen to their excuses and hope that the tenant sorts out their problems in time to meet the following month's rent. However, situations like this rarely correct themselves and you can find yourself three months in arrears before deciding to take action.

The main type of eviction notice, and the one most commonly used, is a **section 21 notice**. This will give the landlord possession of a property and can be served to the tenants at any time during the tenancy.

However, a landlord can only regain possession of the property at the *end* of the assured short-hold agreement.

If a landlord wants to regain possession *before* the tenancy agreement ends, a **section 8 notice** must be served on the basis that the tenants have breached the agreement. This would be, for example, where the tenant has not paid the rent on time. This notice will explain to the tenants why the landlord is seeking to repossess the property.

The tenants have 14 days to respond to a section 8 being served. If the tenant hasn't responded within the 14 days, you should issue legal proceedings straightaway, lodging an application at the county court requesting an order for repossession of your property. Once the application is lodged it can take about four to six weeks for a hearing date. At this court hearing the landlord will be required to produce a copy of the tenancy agreement, and explain the details regarding the breach of the agreement and any arrears. If all goes according to plan, the judge will inform the tenant that they have 14 days to vacate the property. If things do not go so well, the judge may extend the time the tenant has to vacate the property to four or five weeks. In most cases, tenants will move out as instructed. If they decide to outstay their welcome and ignore the judge's order then a further application will have them removed by a county court bailiff. This is quite uncommon and most tenants will vacate the property before the court hearing.

In order to avoid this situation arising, as mentioned earlier it's crucial to reference your tenants at the start of the tenancy agreement. I always try to obtain an employment reference, which should provide an indication of the tenant's ability to pay the rent. If you want to avoid going through the eviction process yourself, then you can call in an eviction service company to handle the process on your behalf. In this case you should be billed in stages appropriate to the circumstances.

SUMMING UP

There are advantages and disadvantages to managing your own properties, and to using a letting agent to rent your properties. There may be times when it makes sense to let an agent manage and rent your properties for you and vice versa.

Should you decide to use a letting agent or management company, do your homework and make sure you are using a reputable company.

When managing yourself, make certain to take out the necessary checks on your tenants and prepare all the necessary paperwork, including a thorough tenancy agreement. Always go the extra mile and ensure your properties are well maintained and prepared properly for your tenants.

STEP 6.

DEVELOPING YOUR PORTFOLIO

INTRODUCTION

ONCE YOU HAVE a few properties under your belt and have begun to enjoy the experience of owning income-generating buy-to-let property, you may want to take your business further. This brings us back to strategy again.

There are three scales of property investors. There are the part-time, small-scale investors who own one to five buy-to-let properties. These investors tend to manage their portfolios in their spare time.

Then there are the more serious mid-scale investors who own up to 20 properties. These investors tend to try and run their portfolios with the help of others whilst still employed or holding down another job.

Lastly, there are the full-time, large-scale investors who own more than 20 properties. These more serious investors usually set up a company to operate and manage their portfolio and employ staff to help run their business.

In this chapter we will look at how to go from being the first kind of investor to the second kind – how to go from five properties, in other words, to 20, and to create serious long-term passive income. From there to the third scale, is usually just a matter of time. For the sake of this explanation I will refer to the small-scale part-time investor as the 'part-time investor' and the more serious mid-scale investor as the 'professional investor'.

Buy it, Let it, Keep it

There are three basic ways of dealing in property. These are:

1. Buy it, flip it, sell it.
This means buying a property off-plan and selling it or assigning your interest in the property to another buyer before completion – therefore never having legally owned the property.

Example: you buy a property off-plan for £200,000, putting down a 5% deposit of £10,000. Twelve months later, before the property is fully built, property prices have risen 10%. You decide to sell (in this case 'flip') the property through a local estate agent. In order to assign the contract to the buyer, the buyer pays you the appreciated value of 10% = £20,000 + your 5% deposit = £10,000, a total of £30,000.

2. Buy it, complete, and sell it.
With this strategy you purchase the same property for £200,000, putting down a 5% deposit (£10,000) on exchange of contracts and another 5% (£10,000) on completion. Then, once completed, you put the house back on the market for £220,000 and sell it. You receive £20,000 (the appreciated value) and your £20,000 deposit.

3. Buy it, let it, keep it.
This strategy just does exactly what it says. And it's my strategy of choice. This is probably the most sustainable way to scale up as a property investor, as it increases your portfolio without requiring ever more intensive short-term work in endlessly selling property.

Buying, letting, keeping also allows you to use built-up equity to build your portfolio: you can borrow money to buy future properties based on the increased value of properties you already hold. It is very hard to beat this approach to becoming a property investor.

I know some people who simply buy and sell property with a view to making a quick profit and have no intention of owning or building a portfolio (see 1 and 2 above). While I don't think this is as stress-free or long-term a prospect as buying, letting and keeping, it is a method that could be used to build yourself enough profit to purchase property with a view to keeping it for the long term.

FROM PART-TIME INVESTOR TO PROFESSIONAL INVESTOR

If you decide to expand you property portfolio, you need a good strategy. As I wrote earlier, when I began investing in property I was in it purely for capital gain, as are most who start out as property investors. In other words, I only cared about making money by selling a property for more than I bought it for.

Those who do invest for cash flow tend to be the more experienced investor looking for rental returns that are higher than their outgoings (including mortgage payments).

Investing just for a capital gain is all well and good when the market is stable and appreciating in value. But it misses a huge part of what's on the table even then. And, of course, we all know now that the market simply *isn't* always stable and appreciating in value.

CASH FLOW AND CAPITAL GAIN

Pursuing capital gain *and* cash flow is important for expanding a property portfolio because it is a strategy that can survive downturns and it also opens up greater opportunities for growing your income.

So the reasons I changed my strategy in 2008 were twofold. Firstly, this change was forced upon me by stagnating house prices and the economic downturn of 2007. Secondly, after years of growing a property portfolio where I owned more than ten properties, I finally came to the conclusion that I wasn't taking advantage of a big opportunity to grow my income.

> **Property investment should be part of a wealth-creation strategy, not just a speculative purchase or two in isolation.**

My new strategy was to grow a large asset base and then enjoy the positive cash flow it provided.

I realised that one, two or even three properties generating positive cash flow from reliable tenants might not make much difference to my lifestyle or my ability to acquire further property, but five to ten properties providing a healthy return *could* make that difference.

It's important to understand that great wealth from property investment is achieved through *long-term* capital appreciation and the ability to refinance to buy further properties, as well as a positive cash flow generated from your portfolio.

Once I realised this, I was able to set out a new five year strategy to refinance, by borrowing extra capital from existing properties, to build my portfolio from ten properties up to 15.

I knew that once I had achieved this goal and was experiencing a much-improved positive cash-flow, I would want to build my portfolio up to a point where I was generating enough income (over and above my expenses/outgoings) to live off, without having to rely on my nine-to-five day job.

That shifts the emphasis onto rental yield for money that I live off, rather than capital gain. But the capital gain still exists, accumulating quietly, building over the long term until such a time as I want to sell.

How many properties you need to own to be in a position to give up the day job is determined by different factors, such as how much rental income you have over and above your expenses, and how much income you need to live off each year. **I believe that figure to be somewhere between ten and 20 properties, depending on these factors.**

GEARING AND INCREASING THE SIZE OF YOUR PORTFOLIO

Some might argue that if you never sell any property, you never realise the capital gain the property has made over so many years, and therefore you can never enjoy the benefit of that gain.

However, *the more property you own the more passive income you create.* And the more you can borrow from the equity those properties hold, the more property you can purchase, creating even more income.

Example 1: Increasing your portfolio from two to four properties using built-up equity

Joe purchases two buy-to-let properties, each worth £140,000, totalling £280,000, and puts in a 15% deposit for each property.

- Two properties worth £280,000.
- Deposit paid (15%) = £42,000.
- Mortgage loan = £238,000 (interest only).

Now let's move forward three years and assume the value of the properties has increased 6% each year during those three years.

- Two properties now worth £333,000.
- Deposit paid (15%) = £42,000.
- Mortgage loan = £238,000 (interest only).

After three years Joe now has £95,000 equity, has realised a gain of £53,000 and the running cost of the properties has been paid for by the tenants' rent.

The mortgage loan and the amount Joe has invested have stayed the same but Joe has now reaped a healthy profit and can go back to his lender to borrow another £46,000 or more from the built up equity to purchase another two properties. This means Joe takes his borrowing up from £238,000 to £284,000, still leaving £49,000 equity (15%) in the properties.

Now Joe has four properties without having to put in any more of his own money but using the gain he has made from the original two properties he purchased. These two new properties Joe purchases (property 3 and 4), are bought for £160,000 each, totalling £320,000 and pays a 15% deposit totalling £48,000 out of his capital gain.

- Four properties now worth £653,000.
- Original deposit paid = £42,000.
- Mortgage loan = £510,000.

After another three years and 6% growth in property prices, Joe now has:

- Four properties worth £777,000.
- Original deposit paid = £42,000.
- Mortgage loan = £510,000.

Six years have passed since Joe purchased his first two properties using £42,000 of his own money. In that time he has increased his portfolio to four properties now worth £777,000. He may owe a large amount to the bank (£510,000), but he is now sitting on £267,000 equity – not a bad return for six years and a £42,000 investment. The other positive outcome is that Joe's gearing is now 65% instead of 85% and he enjoys the added bonus of a healthy rental income.

Example 2: Increasing your rental gain at the same time as increasing your portfolio from five to eight properties using built-up equity

John owns five houses, returning £10,000 each in rental income a year. That's £50,000 a year.

John's annual costs are £28,000, including mortgage payments, repairs and renewals, and management costs (£25,000 in mortgage interest payments + £3,000 for running costs). John's total income after expenses is £22,000.

John then decides to invest and develop his portfolio, increasing the number of properties he owns to eight, but he doesn't have the money to invest further so he goes to his mortgage lender and asks to increase his borrowing by releasing some of the equity that has built up in his first few purchased properties. He has these properties valued and some of them have risen in value to bring his LTV (loan to value) down to approximately 60%.

For the sake of this explanation, and to try and keep it simple, lets say John's five properties are valued at a total of £800,000 (£160,000 each), and his borrowing is currently £500,000. The bank or mortgage lender will lend him another £100,000, taking his LTV or gearing up to 75%.

So with this newly raised £100,000 capital, let's say John purchases another three properties valued at £150,000 each (20% deposit + purchasing costs), using an average of £33,000 for each property (£30,000 deposit + £3,000 purchasing costs).

John has now created another £30,000 annual rental income (£10,000 rental income from each), at the same time as creating extra annual costs of £23,000 (£18,000 for the three new mortgages of £120,000 each at a 5% interest only rate) + £5,000 interest on the £100,000 extra, borrowed from the equity from the original five properties. So he now has an annual income from eight properties of £80,000 a year and costs of £51,000 (£28,000 from the original five properties + £23,000 for the three new properties).

Five properties = £800,000 (averaging £160,000 each)

Rental income = £50,000 a year − costs of £28,000
Income − costs = £22,000

Eight properties = £1,280,000 a year (averaging £160,000 each)

Rental income = £80,000 a year − costs of £51,000
Income − costs = £29,000

> **TIP:** Gearing
>
> I do not like to have a gearing of higher than 75%. I believe it's important to have a safety cushion of 25% equity, allowing for a sudden drop in property prices or a severe downturn in the economy. After the economic collapse of 2007/2008, and witnessing the financial devastation brought on for so many people who were too highly leveraged, I decided to always give myself a 25% cushion for any similar future occasion.

Now John has increased his portfolio from five properties to eight properties. If each property is valued at £160,000 (the three new acquisitions were bought at £10,000 BMV – below market value), the portfolio is now worth £1,280,000 with borrowing of £960,000. John now has equity of £320,000 up from £250,000 and increased annual rental income. Another thing to consider is this: if property prices rise by 5%, the following year John will be £64,000 better off instead of £40,000 (when he owned five properties).

- 2013: five properties worth £800,000
- 2014: five properties worth £840,000 (with a 5% increase in prices)
- **Gain of £40,000**
- 2013: eight properties worth £1,280,000
- 2014: eight properties worth £1,344,000 (with a 5% increase in prices)
- **Gain of £64,000**

I am obviously using these figures purely for the purposes of explanation, but hope you can see how this strategy can work to grow your property portfolio at the same time as creating a healthy positive cash flow.

The more property you own, the more income is generated.

With the right strategy in place – and provided you are doing the appropriate homework on each and every property you invest in – you can create a fantastic return on that investment.

You can then decide to take it to the next stage and borrow again from equity in some of the earlier properties you purchased to invest further. Certain doom-mongers will tell you that you are borrowing too much and getting yourself in deep water.

However, what is the difference between owning one property worth £200,000 with a £100,000 mortgage, and owning ten properties worth £2,000,000 with £1,000,000 mortgaged? You still have 50% borrowing and 50% equity – and you are now a property millionaire.

* * *

I once watched one of those many property programmes on TV a few years ago, and remember the interviewer looking aghast when the experienced property investor mentioned he had borrowed £4,000,000.

She was so horrified at this, I don't think she heard the investor tell her a few moments later that his properties were worth a total value of £7,500,000.

What is important here is not that this particular investor had £3,500,000 in equity in his property and was a multi-millionaire, although that in itself is quite important, but that he had between £175,000 and £200,000 rental income each year after expenses from all his property, and that included the cost of having someone else manage his portfolio for him.

This great accumulation of wealth and property didn't happen overnight and didn't arise through luck or chance. This particular investor had spent some 15 or 16 years amassing a property portfolio worth £7.5m. When the interviewer asked him if he slept sound at night having £4m mortgaged, his reply came with a wry smile, "Wouldn't you if you knew you had more than £3m in equity and an income of £200,000 a year?"

But none of this struck me as much as his comment a little later, when asked what he does with his time now. This man was in his 40s or 50s and through his own endeavour had created a life where he was free to spend his time however he wanted.

He explained that he mostly spent time looking for property deals and ways in which to grow his business. What I heard was that he was *free* … free to do whatever he wanted, whenever he wanted, and didn't need to concern himself with the responsibility of a nine-to-five day job, nor worry about future income during his retirement years. I envisaged a time, perhaps ten years later, when his property empire would be worth £14m with rental income in the region of £350,000 to £400,000 a year.

I assumed at this point in time this particular investor could choose to sell some of his properties to purchase whatever he wanted. But then why would he have to sell anything when he was earning £350,000–400,000 a year? It all stacked up for me then. It made so much sense. I couldn't understand why more people didn't follow the same path in life.

The more I thought about it, the more I realised that like so many successful people in life, this young man had a plan that had arisen from a vision and goals that he had set himself. And that for me was the reason why so many people hadn't followed this path. It was the thought that this would all take too long, require too much forethought and too much hard work.

People want success now and without all the effort and planning that goes into bringing about prosperity years later.

At a recent property investment meeting I attended, an older gentleman with 100 buy-to-let properties to his name was talking about buying and selling. This very experienced property investor suggested that one should never sell an investment property that is making money. He asked the question: why would you sell an asset that provides a good income? If you decide to sell that property you become liable for capital gains tax. Sometimes it can be necessary – personal circumstances change, or you may need extra capital to invest in another property – but it's much *less* necessary than the majority of property investors realise.

CASE STUDY: Selling and CGT vs remortgaging

For years I believed that I would sell a particular property we owned once it reached a certain value, in order to pay off the mortgage on our family home or re-invest it in other properties.

On a few occasions I did come close to selling this property simply because there was £200,000 equity in it, and I believed I could put that equity to much better use elsewhere. However, whenever I came close to selling it the figures just didn't make sense. In particular, selling this property would leave me faced with a CGT bill of 28% – approximately £50,000 (after CGT relief).

I decided that the best strategy was to re-mortgage the property to release the equity. At the time the house was valued at £400,000 and the mortgage on the property was £200,000 (I had previously re-mortgaged the property).

The bank was willing to lend me another £80,000 (70% LTV). Now there are a few things to think about with this scenario, so let's break it down into the positives and negatives to gauge whether it made good financial sense.

By borrowing an extra £80,000, I would be increasing the mortgage from £200,000 to £280,000 and therefore my monthly mortgage payments would increase from £833 to £1,166, an increase of £333. (The rental income from this property had been £1,300 a month, rising to £1,400 the following year.)

You could argue that increasing my monthly mortgage payments by £333 is a negative. With this increase I would also have less positive rental income – again, a potential negative.

But, by the same token, I would have less rental income showing on my end-of-year tax return, and therefore would have less tax to pay. A positive.

The most important point is what I do with the extra borrowing. I now have £80,000 with which to purchase one, two or possibly three more properties, depending on how much deposit I wish to put down. Personally, I would try to purchase as many as possible. Perhaps three houses for £150,000, each with 15% down, leaving myself with approximately £10,000–12,000 for legal costs, furnishings, any repairs or renewals etc. This is definitely a positive.

This property will certainly rise in value again in the next few years, and I might be in a position to borrow against it later on, releasing even more equity. It definitely makes more sense to avoid the hefty capital gains tax for selling the property, and instead re-mortgage the property to release further equity.

TIP: Tax

Never try to pay off or lower the amount you owe on a buy-to-let mortgage. If you have a £100,000 interest-only mortgage on a property worth £150,000, and ten years later the property has doubled in value to £300,000, then you are far better off re-mortgaging and releasing another £50,000 equity with which to purchase another property. This means your mortgage will still only be half the value of your property and you will be limiting the amount of tax you will be liable for at the end of the tax year.

CASE STUDY: Selling to invest

It can make sense to sell a property if you are going to use the profit/equity to invest in other property. Some years ago we moved out of our family home for a short period as we had decided to carry out some extensive building improvements, involving a big extension and six to seven months' renovation work.

I didn't like the thought of renting and began looking for another property to buy, but this time with a view to living in it and then selling it once we relocated back to our family home. My wife thought I was completely mad, but I did have a plan.

I found a property in poor condition that was in need of a full renovation. It was on the market for £245,000 so I offered £220,000. The vendor was not desperate to sell, so I thought there might be a period of haggling and negotiating ahead of us. My initial thoughts were that I might get it for £225,000.

One thing in our favour was that we had a few months before the work was due to start on our house. This meant we had time to find a suitable house to live in and our builders were fairly flexible with dates for starting the project. This was the clincher. The vendor had little interest from anyone else and was expecting us to eventually come back with a revised offer.

The estate agent had advised us that the vendor wanted nearer £230,000 and I was tempted to increase our offer to £225,000. I went back to view the house for a second time and calculated that £20,000 would be required to put the property in order and make it habitable.

I also felt that we could delay a further offer a little longer. Sure enough, two or three weeks later and with no other interested parties, the agent called to say the vendor would accept our initial offer of £220,000.

We spent a total of £25,000 refurbishing this house, lived in it for seven months and sold it two months later after moving out for £272,000. This gave us a profit of £27,000 after expenses, not a bad return after nine months. Why did we sell this property and not keep it for the long term and as a buy-to-let investment? Because this was our primary residential home for the duration of owning the property so there was no capital gains tax to pay. Had we kept the property and then rented it out, it would then have become liable for CGT.

As luck would have it we sold this property in 2006, and we all know what happened to the property market at the back end of 2007. Not only would we have missed out on £27,000 profit, free from CGT, we would probably not have been in a position to sell that house for any profit between 2007 and 2013.

The point of these two differing case studies is that there is no single way to go about your personal financial strategy and the long-term planning of your portfolio. Flexibility is important: respond to each opportunity or demand as is best for that particular opportunity or demand. Don't get fixated on one way of doing things. If you're thorough in your thinking, you shouldn't go wrong.

I always find it helps to write things down on paper. I go with two or three different solutions and their possible outcomes and follow them through, year one, year two, year three and so on. This does not always give me the answers but it does help to clarify things in my mind, and lets me see things from a different perspective.

It is paramount to have a strategy and to constantly review that strategy. There is no problem *changing* your strategy – I have over the years. But you must constantly review in which direction you wish to go and how to go about getting there. It will keep you on target.

POSITIVE CASH FLOW STRATEGY

So how do we go about creating a positive cash flow when buying investment property?

To begin with you must do the maths. You can't purchase a three-bed house for £250,000 that commands a monthly rental of £1,000 and hope to create a positive cash flow. If you put in a 15% deposit of £37,500 leaving a mortgage of £212,500 your monthly interest payments at 5% will be about £900. Add in other expenses such as buildings insurance, repairs and renewals, letting agents fees and allowing for void periods, and you will end up with negative cash flow.

On the other hand, if it's a four-bed house and you can get a monthly rental of £1,500 then the figures will stack up, creating a positive cash flow.

Different towns command different rental incomes. I live in a suburb of south Manchester, where a three-bed semi can command a monthly rental of between £900 and £1,000, yet a similar property just one mile down the road, in an area that attracts a lot of students and young professionals, will typically fetch only £800 to £900 a month.

You would think it makes more sense to purchase the property that commands the higher monthly rental – but the property prices where I live are typically 30–40% more expensive.

When I did the research I found that this area one mile down the road, popular with students and young professionals, was an ideal place to invest in.

Area A	Area B
Three-bed semi £170,000	Three-bed semi £230,000
20% deposit = £34,000	20% deposit = £46,000
Monthly rent = £850	Monthly rent = £950
Mortgage payment (interest-only at 5%) = £566	Mortgage payment (interest-only at 5%) = £766
Income after expenses = £284	Income after expenses = £184

In the case above there are a few further things to consider.

1. Area A is an ideal area for rentals and therefore will have fewer void periods.

2. A much lower deposit and lower investment will be needed to purchase the property in Area A.

3. After expenses/outgoings, Area A will give you a better return on your investment with a higher monthly income.

Similar sorts of comparisons can, and should, be drawn up for any number of competing areas when you're looking for properties.

There will be other things to consider – such as whether a property requires any additional investment for a new kitchen or bathroom, for new carpets, furniture and so on – but that applies to any property in any area. The foregoing figures are only comparing one area with another when trying to decide which property will return a *positive cash flow*.

CASE STUDY: Weighing up several properties

Recently I was faced with a tough decision about which property to go for. Three potential investment properties came onto the market, all in areas I would invest in. I believed they offered good potential for capital growth and rental income. All three properties in three different areas were priced below market value, and one was a repossession.

The repossession was a two-bed flat for sale at £65,000 (£110,000 market value), one was a three-bed house at £142,000 that I thought I could get for £135,000 (£170,000 market value) and one was a new build available at £105,000 (£125,000 market value).

It looked obvious to me at the time that the two-bed flat made more sense to purchase, taking cash flow and capital gain into consideration, but when I spread the properties out side by side on an A4 piece of paper and took all the figures into account (such as rental income, mortgage costs, capital growth) and worked out my return on investment, it wasn't so clear cut.

In fact, there wasn't much in it at all. I had wanted to purchase all three properties as I liked the potential with all of them, but finances at the time only allowed me the opportunity to go for one of them. As it happened I did end up opting for the two-bed flat not only because it offered me the best ROI, but also because my financial outlay was going to be a lot lower than for the other two properties.

The three-bedroom house going for £142,000 needed some repairs and renewals, with about £5,000–£7,500 needing to be spent on it, whereas the two-bedroom flat only needed a lick of paint and some furniture to prepare it for renting. A 20% deposit plus expenses meant I had to spend £15,000, whereas had I opted for the three-bed house and managed to get it for £135,000, my outlay would have been at least £35,000 (including stamp duty, legal costs, repairs and renewals and furniture).

At the time of writing, the rental market is booming – as it has been since 2007. The demise of property prices after the boom period meant a surge in rentals during the bust period.

In January 2012, the *Financial Times* reported:

Loans squeeze spurs buy-to-let boom
Private sector landlords have increased their share of residential stock by 42% since 2007 and now account for 19% of the total value. Cash-rich buy-to-let landlords are benefiting from the lack of bank lending to other potential home-owners and the lowest level of housing output since 1923, which has helped drive rental demand and increase yields.

Buy-to-let property used to be a pure play on capital growth, but now you are basically buying rental income with a fairly good guarantee that the underlying asset will also grow in value.

The head of one of the top estate agencies in London, quoted in the *FT* article, forecasted that landlords could own 6.6m houses by 2021, equivalent to 22% of all British homes.

Many investors believe that, though house prices may remain flat for another year or two, strong demand from tenants looking for a place to rent – thus generating positive cash flow – is a big incentive to carry on buying. House prices rising with a return in confidence will then boost capital values.

If this reading of the property cycle is right, these next few years from 2014 onwards are ripe with opportunity.

Rentals are expected to continue growing at about 5–10% a year over the next three to five years. Of course, once property prices start rising again (something I personally believe will happen from 2014–2015), investors will be reaping the rewards of great rental income *and* capital growth.

SUMMING UP

Many property investors usually own between one and five buy-to-let properties and stop there. They feel that taking it to the next level is too big and scary a step to take. My belief is that once you have taken that first step and borrowed money to start your portfolio, realising the potential for long-term financial security, you should find it easier and more comfortable to take it to the next level.

After all, the levels of debt involved may increase – but only entirely in proportion to the levels of equity you'll own and the rental income you'll receive.

The real question is: how many properties do you need to fund the lifestyle you desire?

STEP 7.

BUYING (AUCTIONS AND OFF-PLAN) AND SELLING – THE LONG TERM

INTRODUCTION

THERE WILL COME a time when you decide to sell a property, either to enjoy the rewards of your hard work and to release some capital, or to re-invest the equity built up to purchase more property or other assets. This chapter explains the process for selling property yourself or through an agent.

Many property investors prefer to buy property off-plan or at auctions as opposed to through an estate agent, as they view these as opportunities to pick up a bargain. This chapter will also explain in detail how to prepare for auctions and the different stages involved when bidding for a property. Buying off-plan can be risky but rewarding. Providing you do your research first, and your timing is right, you can pick up some really good deals.

SELLING YOUR PROPERTY THROUGH AN AGENT

DISHES IN THE BEDROOMS

If you do decide to sell one of your buy-to-let properties you should sell it empty rather than tenanted.

Some landlords try to sell a property when it has tenants on a short-term tenancy agreement, as they feel it will attract landlords looking to benefit from rental income as soon as they take ownership. This *can* work: I once purchased a property that had existing tenants who had another six months left on their tenancy agreement. What appealed to me was the fact the tenants were paying very high rent and and were all in full-time employment.

I was getting the property for a good price, I liked its location – the fact I was going to benefit from just under £9,000 rental income in six months was simply the icing on the cake.

But this situation is unusual.

Any other time I have viewed property for sale with tenants, I have turned it down. In nearly all cases I have found the property in a complete mess, with clothes strewn all over the place, dirty pots and pans in the kitchen sink and in the living room, and in some cases also in the bedrooms.

The furniture is nearly always ripped and stained, and the garden is usually overgrown and unkempt. It isn't difficult to be turned off a property when you see it in such a state.

So I would advise waiting for your tenants to move out once the tenancy agreement has terminated, and then spending some money redecorating the property to ensure it is in saleable condition. If it means spending an extra £1,000 putting in some new furniture and new curtains it will be money well spent and will probably ensure you sell your property a lot quicker.

GETTING THE RIGHT VALUE

Decide what price you want to achieve for your property before approaching any estate agents. Check websites and local agents to see if any similar properties are for sale in the same road or on nearby roads.

I would recommend talking to *three* estate agents and asking them all to value your property with a view to selling it. Most agents will want to secure the contract and in some cases will over-value your property believing you will opt for the agent with the highest valuation. This is one reason it is important for you to do the research and have a price in mind as to what you believe the property is worth.

If you believe your property is worth £200,000 and two of the agents value it within £10,000 of that price, then you will know you are fairly accurate in your estimation. If the third agent values it at £230,000 and gives you lots of good reasons why they believe they can sell it for this price, *you should be sceptical and doubt their sincerity.*

It is sometimes difficult to know which agent to choose, so trust your intuition and go with your gut feeling if unsure. They will certainly want you to sign a sole agency agreement meaning they have exclusivity on selling your property, in which case ask for and read their terms and conditions. On one occasion, when I decided to sell a property, the agent I opted for had a clause in their terms and conditions charging £150 for terminating the contract. This meant that if they were unsuccessful selling my property and I decided take it off the market or give it to another agent, I would have to have paid them for the privilege. There were other clauses I didn't like and asked them to change them before signing the contract. And they did change them.

I think three to six months is a reasonable period of time to give any agent the opportunity to sell your property, so ensure you do not sign any terms and conditions that tie you in for longer than this.

COMMISSION

Estate agent commission rates can vary hugely – from as little as 1% to as much as 4%. This commission rate is normally negotiable, so try to negotiate as low a rate as possible, and once agreed ask for confirmation in writing.

City-centre agents tend to charge a higher commission rate than smaller out-of-town agents – somewhere between 2.5% and 4% – and usually won't budge on their fees. Out-of-town agents seem to be happier to negotiate and tend to have lower commission rates of 1–2.5%.

You should ask the agent to see the property description and photos before they begin marketing. They may omit some important information or perhaps have included some poor quality photos. When selling one property, I noticed that the agent had included a photo of the front garden full of rubbish and beer cans. I was astounded that the person taking the photos hadn't bothered removing the rubbish beforehand.

Also, ask to see a sales brochure so you can see the quality of marketing information they provide for potential buyers. Check to see what papers and what websites they advertise on, and then look it up afterwards to make sure it's showing. Most agents, if not all, should have your property featured on **www.rightmove.co.uk**.

SELLING YOUR PROPERTY YOURSELF

Selling your property yourself can save you thousands of pounds. Obviously, using an agent has its benefits and will save you time. However, it can be costly.

It's important to set the right price for your property, so I recommend asking three local agents to value your property and doing some research yourself. Check out other similar properties for sale and use websites such as **www.rightmove.co.uk** and **www.houseladder.co.uk** to see what similar houses have sold for in your area in the last year or two.

There are many websites you can advertise your property on, including **www.propertysell.co.uk**, **www.houseladder.co.uk** and **www.houseswift.co.uk**. I would also recommend taking out an ad in the local papers as well as a national daily in their property section. Spread the word amongst friends and work colleagues and let as many people as possible know you have a property for sale. If you belong to a local property networking group, make all the members aware and ask them to spread the word.

Get a local sign-maker to make you a *For Sale* sign; this should only cost between £30 and £40. It's probably worth calling the local council to ask them if there is a maximum size board you can erect.

Prepare some sales leaflets with a good and thorough description of the property. Use an estate agent's copy as a guideline but avoid using the estate agent jargon: keep it simple with photos and correct room dimensions. If you don't have the skills to put this together yourself, ask a local printing company to help. Make sure you include your mobile number so potential buyers can contact you to arrange viewings.

Have a list of questions prepared when interested parties call you. Questions you should ask are:

- Do you have a property to sell?
- Do you know the area or are you from this area?
- How quickly do you want to move?
- Do you have finance in place?

It's important to find out as much as you can about any potential buyer and by asking such questions you will be able to tell how serious they are before they view your property. Once you have this information you can then arrange a viewing happy that you have done some research on your potential purchaser.

They will probably have plenty of questions for you so be well-prepared and make certain you have all the details about the property to hand. Is the property a leasehold or freehold? If it's a leasehold, how long is left on the lease? How much is the monthly service charge? Is there a designated car parking space? How much are the utility bills?

Be prepared for negotiation on the price and have in mind the lowest price you are prepared to accept. Once you have agreed a price, you should exchange solicitor details and let them carry out the paperwork and exchange and completion contracts.

Also, bear in mind that even after you have agreed a price with the purchaser, they might try and haggle further after the survey. A survey can throw up some problems that might need attending to and the purchaser may feel that they can negotiate a lower price through their solicitor.

If this happens you need to decide whether you are prepared to negotiate further. This happened to me some years ago when a survey on one of properties showed up some problems with a flat roof above the kitchen. The surveyor pointed out that the flat roof was badly in need of repair and might cost in the region of £1,000–£2,000 to replace. There were other less serious issues and the surveyor valued my property £3,000–£4,000 less than the sale amount we had agreed.

The sale amount was £76,000 and we had agreed to sell for £75,000, but after the survey the purchaser revised his offer down to £71,000. I decided to stand firm and initially wouldn't budge on the price agreed. However, after a lot of haggling and a second face-to-face meeting, I agreed to drop the price to £74,000 and the deal was done. I decided that the purchaser had a genuine cause for concern, and because neither of us had anticipated a lower valuation on the property, I felt it was fair to take something off the agreed price.

BUYING AT AUCTIONS

I am not a big fan of buying at auctions in the early stages of becoming a property investor, but you can certainly benefit greatly from buying at an auction if you do your homework.

If you are a novice at buying property and have yet to experience the hustle and bustle of auctions, I strongly recommend visiting a few before you decide to start bidding against other experienced investors.

All sorts of properties are sold at auction, including flats, houses, commercial and residential property. Many of the properties on offer are being offloaded by the council or housing association, who will take the best price on the day. Other properties on offer can be probate sales, or simply a property that someone is in a rush to sell. A probate sale is where the owner of the property has passed away and the property is being sold by the executor of the will or a family member (if there is no will).

Most buyers at an auction are developers or builders who are looking for a good deal with a view to renovating and selling for a quick profit. There will also be those who are looking for a project, someone interested in doing up a property and a total renovation for themselves to live in or sell on.

REPOSSESSIONS

More than 20% of all residential properties offered at property auctions are repossessions. The banks who repossessed them want speedy sales and investors want to grasp them. Estate agents have recently started calling repossessions by another term: corporate sales.

Because there have been so many repossessions in recent years due to the economic downturn, there are many opportunities out there for the seasoned investor. Providing you do your homework there are some incredible gains to be made when purchasing repossessions.

I prefer to buy in town or city centres where demand for rentals is strong. In this case you can benefit from good yields (how much of an annual return you are likely to get from your investment – calculated by expressing a year's rental income as a percentage of how much the property cost) and good rental returns. Again, it's important to stress that you should do as much research as possible before bidding for a repossession. View the property first, and make sure you are buying with vacant possession.

When you feel you are ready to buy at an auction, ask the company holding the auction for their catalogue and decide what properties you are most interested in. Viewing these properties is important and can be made through the auctioneer.

Two of the largest auction companies are Allsop & Co. (**www.allsop.co.uk**) and Pugh (**www.pugh-auctions.com**). If you register with them they will email you their monthly catalogue.

DO'S AND DONT'S FOR BUYING AT AUCTIONS

CHECK THE LEGAL DOCUMENTATION

Check through all available paperwork and find out as much as you can about the property. There should be some legal documentation, including the condition of sale. Having visited the property, and if you are still keen to purchase it, then get your solicitor to check out the legal documentation to ensure there are no problems with the title deeds.

VISIT THE PROPERTY BEFORE THE AUCTION

Always visit any property you are thinking of buying at auction and take a builder with you to give you an estimate of how much it will cost to put everything right. You might only have four weeks between when the catalogue is available and the auction, so you will need to act quickly.

CARRY OUT A SURVEY

Instruct a surveyor to carry out a home-buyer's report. If there is any structural damage you will need to know exactly what is involved and how much it's going to cost to fix. A home-buyer's report may cost you £300 to £400. You will be out of pocket for this if you are unsuccessful in purchasing the property, but it's better to lose £400 being scrupulous and putting your mind at rest, than to 'save' it by not carrying out a survey and buying a property that is structurally unsound.

BIDDING – SET A PRICE LIMIT AND STICK TO IT

It's easy to get carried away when bidding, so make sure you have a maximum price in mind that you are prepared to bid up to and *stick to it*. Once the adrenaline is flowing and other interested parties are bidding, you can suddenly get carried along with the excitement of it all and feel that it's a great property with a lot of potential because there is other interest in it.

This is a surefire way to overpay.

I have spoken with many investors who in the heat of the moment have overbid to win a property, and then wished they hadn't. Remember, once the hammer falls, if you are the highest bidder, you are *legally committed to paying the price you bid and completing the sale.*

THE GUIDE PRICE

The guide price is simply what price the property should realise at auction. This will be the price the auctioneer puts in the catalogue, but the actual selling price can be far higher or lower than the guide price, so do not pay *too* much attention to this.

THE RESERVE PRICE

The reserve price is the lowest price the seller will accept. If the bidding doesn't reach the reserve price, the property is withdrawn.

ARRANGE YOUR MORTGAGE BEFORE THE AUCTION

Because you will only have 28 days to complete after the auction, it is important to arrange your mortgage before the auction. If for any reason you are unable to arrange a mortgage after the auction and therefore unable to proceed with the purchase, you will have to forego your 10% deposit. Never bid on a property without having previously arranged your mortgage.

HAVE YOUR DEPOSIT AND PROOF OF ID WITH YOU

You will need a 10% deposit with you and at least two forms of ID before you can exchange contracts. You will also have to pay the auction administration fee.

AUCTION COSTS

The auctioneer may demand a buyer's premium – usually 1.5% of the sale price. There will also be an administration fee, which can be anything from £150 to £600 paid to the auctioneer.

TIP: Auctions

I have been to see quite a few properties due to be auctioned where ten or 20 other interested people also turn up. This gives a good indication of significant interest in the upcoming auction. For this reason I believe it is best to try to purchase the property before the auction so you do not get caught up in a bidding war.

There are advantages and disadvantages to buying at auction, but the golden rules amongst all these are: set yourself a highest purchase price and stick to it and make sure you are well prepared and know the property inside out before you bid for it.

BUYING OFF-PLAN

Buying off-plan tends to be very popular in a rising market and for obvious reasons not so popular in a stagnant or declining market. In order to buy off-plan you really need to have fire in your belly and nerves of steel.

Like any investment, there is an element of risk when investing in property, but buying off-plan is taking it to a new level. You are in effect buying a property that hasn't yet been built.

The developer will try to sell you a property showing you a 'plan' with details of the site layout, square footage and specification of the property. There will be a glossy brochure, lots of advertising, and a beautiful show house with all mod cons – fully furnished – to tempt you into buying.

It is difficult to overlook all the glitz and try to see the property as it might look in three, four or five years' time.

If you are buying off-plan in a rising market you can achieve a good discount as you are buying long before the property is built. By the time it is completed, in one or two years' time, the property's value could have risen by as much as 20%.

Again it is important to do the research and ensure you are being offered a good deal. Check out the prices of any similar properties for sale in the area. If you do find anything similar for a lower price, *make a lower offer*; the seller can only reject it. And they might accept your offer if they are not selling as many properties as they had hoped to. If you get in early on in the development you can stand a better chance of getting a discount as the developer may need to secure a few sales in order to start building. You will also get to choose one of the better sites on the development.

Because the properties have not yet been built, it may also be worth negotiating for a higher specification in the property such as wooden floors or granite kitchen work surfaces. The developer might not want to budge on the price of the property – but could be happier throwing in some extras such as free kitchen appliances, or an extra car parking space.

There are all sorts of incentives to be offered to tempt you into buying, ranging from upgraded appliances and furniture packs to free flooring. Other incentives include guaranteed rental packages for a certain period, stamp duty paid, or even a cash-back scheme.

TIP: New developments

Visit a developer at the end of the development to see if there are any remaining properties that haven't sold. This can be a good time to make a low offer and get a good last-minute deal. If the developer is waiting to move off the site and has completed all the building work, he may want to offload the few remaining properties at a reduced price, rather than having the cost of keeping a sales team and sales office on site for longer than needed.

On two different occasions I approached a developer at the end of the development and made an offer for the last remaining unsold properties. Because I was offering to purchase the last two properties that the developer was struggling to sell, I got a great deal and a big discount.

These properties are now rented. On another occasion I purchased a show house from the developer who wanted to rent back the property from me and continue to use it as the show house on the site. They rented the property from me for more than two years, paying a healthy monthly rent six months in advance.

CASE STUDY: Price reductions from developers

I once purchased the last two remaining apartments at a reduced price from a developer as he needed to sell them quickly before moving on to the next stage of the development. Apparently they had already sold these apartments to another investor but the sale fell through towards the end of the process and now the developer was in a hurry to move them on and happy to take a reduced price.

They were for sale at £147,500 and I offered £240,000 for both (£120,000 each). The developer came back and said he would agree to take £125,000 each, but I stood firm because I knew he was in a hurry to sell them.

I had befriended his sales manager and knew that they couldn't begin working on phase two of the development until all the properties from phase one had sold. Two weeks passed and eventually I got the call to say they would agree to my offer of £120,000.

The year was 2007, and because of where we were on the property cycle, I accepted the fact I was taking a risk buying at this time.

Sure enough, soon after buying these apartments property prices did start to decline and we moved into the next stage of the property cycle. Six years later, those two apartments are probably worth what I paid for them or perhaps slightly more. When I purchased them I realised I was taking a risk, but I knew I would have no problem renting the apartments and that even with a 10% drop in prices I would still be in profit.

TIP: Buying

Never buy any property above or at true market value in case prices drop and you end up in negative equity. Always try to buy below market value – if you can't, then don't buy.

Make sure you are buying from a reputable developer who has built other developments. You can then check these out to see the standard of the building work.

If you are buying an apartment off-plan, make sure you read all the paperwork and ask how much the annual service charge will be. Other questions to ask are:

- Is it freehold or leasehold?
- How long is the leasehold?
- Who will the managing agent be once the developer hands it over?
- Will there be a parking space assigned to each apartment?

There are many things to consider when buying off-plan and each development will be different. There is, however, a normal procedure when buying off-plan and all developers should follow this:

RESERVATION FEE

Once you have decided which property or plot you want to purchase you will be asked to pay a reservation or holding fee of anything between £1,000 and £3,000. This is non-refundable.

SOLICITORS

Sometimes the developer will have their own solicitor and insist that they act for both parties involved, appeasing you with discounted legal fees. Otherwise you can use your own preferred solicitor, who will act in your best interests.

INSURANCE

Make sure the developer is NHBC or registered with Zurich. This means the developer is insured against lost deposits and will have to build to certain standards. This will also mean your property will be covered for two years against any snagging issues and ten years for any structural issues.

DEPOSIT
You will be required to pay a 5–10% deposit on exchange of contracts.

COMPLETION
The developer will set a completion date target, but they can and usually will fall behind schedule. Obviously it's in the developers interest to complete the property as planned so as to get paid on time, but if they are delayed you just have to be patient and wait.

HAND-OVER
The developer should keep you up to date with their progress. If they don't then it's in your interest to pester them to find out when completion might take place. They should notify you two weeks before completion, and you will need to be available for the hand-over. Don't plan a holiday or a work trip around the time the developer is expected to complete.

STAMP DUTY
Stamp duty is payable on completion and will be included in the completion paperwork details provided by your solicitor.

SNAGGING
You should be invited to the property during the two-week notice period before completion to draw up a list of snagging issues. The developer is obliged to put any snagging issues right for up to two years after completion.

* * *

Buying off-plan can be risky. If you buy at the end of the property cycle when prices start to fall or become stagnant, you may end up with a property that is worth less when built a year or two after agreeing to purchase it.

If you are intending to flip it, selling it before it is built and before completion, you may end up making a loss or having to rent it because you are unable to sell it for a profit. The only time you should agree a price on a property that hasn't yet been built is when you are confident that the price of the property will be higher once it is completed.

SUMMING UP

Whether you are selling a property yourself or through an agent, make sure you get at least three valuations first. This will give you a good idea as to the real value of your property, ensuring an agent isn't trying to pull the wool over your eyes.

Even if you are giving your property to an agent to sell, do the market research yourself and look up what prices similar properties in the area have sold for. Ask to see the agent's terms and conditions and don't be afraid to challenge them if you are unhappy with any points.

Property investors understand that the best time to make a big profit is from buying below market value. If you end up paying above or even at the true value then you take the risk of ending up in negative equity if prices drop. There are risks involved when buying off-plan or at auctions, but providing you do your homework first there will be opportunities to make a good profit doing so.

CONCLUSION

PROPERTY AND BEYOND

I HAVE WRITTEN this book because I wanted to share with you the knowledge and experience I have gleaned from property investment and because I truly believe that investing in property is a rewarding pursuit at whatever scale it is attempted.

There are also many reasons why I believe now is a good time to invest in property, not least because of where we are on the property cycle.

Experts predicted that there would be a massive drop in house prices after the downturn in the UK economy in 2007. This huge drop in prices – 40% or more – never materialised. Some say house prices are still too high and that the price-to-income ratio is also too high at about five times earnings. Since 2008, this price-to-income ratio has been coming down from a peak high of seven-times earnings, partly as wages have increased a little despite the recession, but mainly because prices have been falling.

But is it right to believe that the ratio should fall below some predetermined level before we can say house prices are at fair value?

Personally, I don't think so – this ratio has been steadily rising for years and the so called 'UK long-term average' or 'natural level' of 3.5 times salary should no longer be the barometer. If you take the latest house price data from Halifax and set it against the UK national mean full-time wage for men (what the ratio was measured by), that ratio average shows that since 1983 the 'natural level' has risen to about 4.2.

Furthermore, the price of a property is now compared with the average earnings of a *household*, as more women are working now than ever before.

Interest rates should also be taken into account. Obviously, interest rates fluctuate – but a first-time buyer can borrow a lot more money at 2% than at 5%, and if you can fix a low rate of say 2% or 3% for five or even ten years then we are talking about a difference of thousands of pounds in repayments.

Another thing to consider is that prices are often set by supply and demand, so if there is a shortage of property with high demand, how can houses be too expensive?

Actually, I believe most banks do not use this multiple of 3.5 any longer. They certainly didn't leading up to the pre-2007 bubble. They will still measure someone's affordability against their salary – as they should – but using a higher multiple of perhaps 4 or 4.5.

Taking all of these figures and factors into consideration, a 'national average' or true level is probably between 4.5 and 5, and since we're around this figure now, I think you could say that British house prices have well and truly 'normalised'.

I hope this book has given you all the knowledge you require and has answered all the questions you might have had so you can begin your journey into property investment. Throughout this book I hope to have convinced you that building and managing a property portfolio is both a wonderful and rewarding experience. If I haven't yet convinced you, below is a recap of why you should take that leap.

LOW BORROWING COSTS

At the time of writing, interest rates are the lowest they've ever been and haven't risen since the latter part of 2007 – seven years ago. This makes borrowing cheap and affordable.

Even when interest rates do rise, it will take years before they reach the levels they were at in 2007. Due to increases in the cost of living in recent years, most people could not afford to pay their monthly mortgage payments if the banks suddenly raised interest rates to the levels they were at in 2007. Interest rates are going to rise at some point, that is certain, but when the banks do start increasing rates they will have to do so slowly.

GROWING POPULATION

There is still a growing population in the UK and a shortfall of property. The population in the UK has risen steadily in the last ten years and continues to rise. Yet developers are building less homes than are needed and the shortfall is growing.

RENTAL GROWTH

Because the banks are tough on lending and building societies want large deposits from first-time buyers, there has never been such massive demand for rentals. In recent years there has been strong growth in the buy-to-let sector, coinciding with the decline in first-time buyers. If you own buy-to-let properties in reasonable condition, you cannot fail to rent out your property. Demand far outstrips supply and will continue to do so for many years to come.

LACK OF OTHER OPTIONS

Other assets, while attractive for some, do not come without problems.

You can't pick up a newspaper at the moment without reading some negative press about pensions. They *can* be a viable and important option, especially given certain tax advantages involved, but there's no guarantee, and fees on pension funds can reduce the value of your pension significantly.

At the same time, changes in how people pay for financial advice mean that getting stock market investment advice will no longer be free upfront (of course, it never was truly free: commissions were paid to the advisor afterwards). This leaves many facing a bewildering array of investment opportunities with little in the way of reliable or affordable guidance.

And, of course, there is no point leaving your money in a bank when interest rates are so low. Any money you do have in the bank is actually decreasing in value thanks to inflation.

SHORTAGE OF PROPERTY

The government realises that there is a huge housing stock shortage in this country, and have been talking about housebuilding programmes to ease the situation. However, very little actual action has been taken.

Meanwhile, a shortage of property and a growing population forces an increase in prices and pushes people into the rental market. Other social forces contribute to this too. There are now more single people living alone in the UK than ever before. With divorce rates increasing, there will be even greater demand for one or two-bed homes in the coming years.

Renting has also become the new way of life for young families who are unable to get on the property ladder.

A SAFE HAVEN

Foreign investors know what they're onto when it comes to British property: overseas buyers have purchased more than 60% of prime property in London in the last few years. Russian, Indian, French and, more recently, Greek and Italian buyers have accounted for *one third of all recent house purchases in central London.* You can guess what effect this has had and will have on property prices.

So why is this? All of these investors see the UK as a safe-haven – a good place to invest their cash. These foreign investors may share a desire for certain aspects of British life, but they are investing in the UK primarily because they believe the future here looks encouraging and because Britain has a strong rule of law and clear tax rules. This bodes well for the property market and the general economy over the coming years.

TAKING ACTION

Imagine no longer needing to work a nine-to-five job, having enough passive income to live off, being free to spend your time how you wish – holidaying, playing golf every day or simply relaxing in your garden.

Well, I hope this book has taught you that this doesn't need to be imaginary. Investing wisely in property for the long term can very much make it a possibility.

Having read this far I hope I have convinced you that investing in property and becoming a landlord is a win-win situation. With the right strategy in place, a little bit of patience and hard work, you can become a property millionaire, benefiting from a healthy income stream. Providing you know what you're doing and carry out good research before diving into the world of property investment, you will be presented with endless opportunities to make money – and lots of it.

Whether you read this book in 2014 when it was published or years later it doesn't matter, the principles are still the same and the property cycle will always be just that, a cycle (a series of events that are regularly repeated in the same order). And throughout this cycle, whether it's year one or year seven, providing we understand the principles and know where we are along the cycle, we are swamped with opportunities. Now is the time to take hold of those opportunities and to make it happen.

Good luck!

RECOMMENDED READING

Here are some of my favourite books – I can't recommend them enough for all property investors. Some are financial, some are about property and some are about motivation.

If you don't like reading, then do try listening to audiobook versions.

GREAT BOOKS FOR PROPERTY INVESTORS

Anyone Can Do It: My Story by Duncan Bannatyne

How to Avoid Property Tax by Carl Bayley

Losing My Virginity: The Autobiography by Richard Branson

How to Win Friends and Influence People by Dale Carnegie

The 7 Habits of Highly Effective People by Stephen Covey

The Power of Intention: Learning to Co-create Your World Your Way by Wayne Dyer

Think Like Da Vinci: 7 Easy Steps to Boosting Your Everyday Genius by Michael Gelb

Feel The Fear And Do It Anyway: How to Turn Your Fear and Indecision into Confidence and Action by Susan Jeffers

Who Moved My Cheese: An Amazing Way to Deal with Change in Your Work and in Your Life by Dr Spencer Johnson

Rich Dad Poor Dad by Robert T. Kiyosaki

Successful Property Letting: How to Make Money in Buy-to-Let by David Lawrenson

Buffett: The Biography by Roger Lowenstein

The Strangest Secret by Earl Nightingale

The Power of Positive Thinking by Norman Vincent Peale

Awaken the Giant within: How to Take Immediate Control of Your Mental, Emotional, Physical and Financial Life by Anthony Robbins

The Millionaire Next Door by Thomas Stanley and William Danko

Goals!: How to Get Everything You Want – Faster Than You Ever Thought Possible by Brian Tracy

Trump: How to Get Rich by Donald Trump

The Psychology of Winning: Ten Qualities of a Total Winner by Denis Waitley

INDEX

A

agents 4, 71-2
 advantages of 78-9
 disadvantage s of 80
 key questions to ask 81
management fees 24, 56, 58, 76, 79, 80
responsibilities 58-9
sales commission 119-20
sales valuations 118-9
selling via 117-20
sole agency agreements 119
sources of information, as 46, 47
trade bodies79
annual exemptions 27-8
Association of Residential Letting
 Agents (ARLA) 79
auctions 122-6
 bidding 124, 126
companies 123
deposits 125
fees 125
guide prices 124-5
ID 125
mortgages, and 125
 paperwork, checking of 123
 repossessions 123
reserve prices 125
 site visits 124
 surveys 124

B

bathrooms 26
Bayley, Carl 28
building insurance, see 'insurance'
building regulations 70-1
buying off-plan 98, 126-131
 completion 130
 considerations 129
 deposits 130
 developer 129
 discounts 126
 handover 130
holding fee 129
insurance, developer's 129
legal team 129
 research 126
reservation fee 129
 specifications 127
 snagging 130
stamp duty 130
timing 127, 130

C

capital
 expenditure 25-6
 gains 21-2, 23, 107-8
 growth 46, 47, 99-100
 improvement, see 'expenditure'
 raising 4

buy-to-let 29-30, 51, 108
  early redemption penalties 31, 34
  fees 29, 34, 51, 56
  fixed-rate 31
  gearing 30, 100-5
  interest-only 31, 34-5
  re-mortgaging 33-4, 52-3, 107-8
  rental potential 29
repayment 31, 34-5
  surveyors 29-30, 34
  tracker 32
  variable 32

N

National Approved Letting Scheme 79
negative equity 20
negotiating 44, 45, 121-2
networking 46, 66-7

O

offer, making an 44
Ombudsman for Estate Agents (OEA)
  59

P

parking 48
planning permission 70-1
population growth 137-8
probate sale 122
property
  availability 138
choosing 47-8, 111-3
overseas investors 138
purchasing costs 53-8
  examples 54, 55

R

references, see 'tenants'
rental
losses 26
potential, see 'mortgages'

return 46
yield 37-9, 47, 123
repairs/renewals 25-6
repossession 21
return on investment (ROI) 39
revenue expenditure 25-6
Rightmove 46, 120

S

section 8 notice 92
section 21 notice 91
selling your property
  tenanted? 117-8
  valuing 118-9, 120
  yourself 120-2
service charges 47, 57
smoke alarms 86
stamp duty (SDLT) 38, 44, 55-6
strategy 7-9, 12
surveys 44-5, 55

T

tax 23-8
  deductibles 25
  income 23, 35-6
  return 22, 23
Tenancy Deposit Scheme (TDS) 78
tenancy agreements
assured short-hold 89, 90, 92
breach of 92
deposits 91
durations 61
excluded tenancy/licence 89
importance of 90-1
joint liability 91
notice 90
pets 90
sample versions 90
tenants, bad 91-2
tenants, finding
  advertising for 59-60